THE BOAT THAT WON THE WAR

An Illustrated History of the Higgins LCVP

THE BOAT THAT WON THE WAR

An Illustrated History of the Higgins LCVP

Charles C Roberts Jr

NAVAL INSTITUTE PRESS
Annapolis, Maryland

Acknowledgements

Special thanks to the following individuals who were consulted and contributed to this work: Robert Jornlin, US Navy Retired; Robert Reeners, WWII coxswain; Alejandro Raigorodsky, Historical Researcher; and Michael Krizsanitz, historian. Renderings by Charles Roberts, John Roberts and Alejandro Raigorodsky.

First published in Great Britain in 2017 by Seaforth Publishing,
an imprint of Pen & Sword Books Ltd,
47 Church Street, Barnsley, South Yorkshire S70 2AS

www.seaforthpublishing.com
info@seaforthpublishing.com

Published and distributed in the United States of America and Canada by the
Naval Institute Press, 291 Wood Road, Annapolis, Maryland 21402-5043
www.nip.org

Library of Congress Cataloging Number: 2017937404

ISBN 978 1 59114 597 4

Designed and typeset by David Rose

Printed by Printworks Global Ltd, London & Hong Kong

CONTENTS

HIGGINS Boats

In Combat

In Commerce

Introduction

Landing craft have been used to support military operations since ancient times. In the *Iliad*, Homer describes how the Greeks sailed across the Aegean Sea, landed on the beaches and attacked the city of Troy. In 490 BC the Persian ruler Darius sent a fleet of ships to attack Greece that included landing craft designed to allow horses to disembark and enter the battle. In 414 BC the Athenian navy put ashore an invasion force to attack the city of Syracuse in Sicily. In 55 BC Julius Caesar landed soldiers on the Kentish coast of Britain. For several decades around 800 AD the Vikings carried out amphibious raids on parts of the British Isles and European coastal areas. The last successful invasion of England came in 1066 when William the Conqueror landed his force on the Sussex coast, defeated the English King Harold at Hastings and established a new blood line of royalty. However, only in very few cases were these operations carried out by specialist landing craft, and history is replete with amphibious landings which were not successful. There was a perception that amphibious landings were risky and often costly. In modern times this was bolstered by the landing operation disaster at Gallipoli in 1915, where British and French troops were initially repulsed at the beach by the Turks. Since amphibious warfare was not part of the military lexicon between the wars, the United States was unprepared for such actions, although the US Navy had not given up totally on amphibious operations and was doing some development work on landing craft in the late 1930s. With the outbreak of the Second World War and the necessity to land forces on foreign coasts, amphibious forces became an important priority for the US Navy. Rapid Japanese conquests in the Far East attested to the viability of amphibious operations. In the early 1940s many American shipyards competed to supply landing craft to the US Navy based on naval designs, but a boat designed and built by Higgins Industries of New Orleans emerged as the best means of putting troops and light vehicles ashore. The evolution of the Higgins design resulted in the Landing Craft Vehicle Personnel (LCVP), or 'Higgins Boat', that General Eisenhower called 'The Boat that Won the War'. Over 23,000 were manufactured and Higgins Boats were used in virtually all US amphibious operations of the Second World War, as well as being supplied in quantity to the Allies. This book reviews the history of the LCVP, the design, the manufacturing, handling and its employment in the Second World War. In terms of significance, the LCVP is one of the most innovative landing craft in naval history.

CHAPTER 1

The Landing Craft Concept

In the late 1930s Andrew Jackson Higgins operated a boatbuilding company in the New Orleans, Louisiana area, specializing in small, versatile, shallow draft watercraft. There was a demand for a small boat that could traverse shallow water and be resistant to propeller damage from floating objects. Trappers and oil company crews needed a vessel to navigate the Louisiana marshes which could run aground, off-load material and back off the shore without hull damage. In response to this need, Higgins Industries developed a wide bow profile boat (pram bow) with a tunnel in the stern to protect the propeller and provide a shallow draft. This was called the Wonderboat. The forebody was round and reinforced to withstand the forces of repeated beachings, and shaped such that the bow wave formed an aerated water surface which tended to reduce hull friction and increase speed. The bow shape also expelled the aerated water to the side, preventing ingestion into the propeller tunnel which would decrease propeller efficiency.

Administration building of the Higgins City Park Plant. (Ref 1. For references see page 128)

Higgins West End Landing Service wharf and showrooms. (Ref 1)

ABOVE
Night view of the City Park Plant, at that time the world's largest building dedicated to the manufacture of naval craft. (Ref 1)

St Charles Avenue plant in New Orleans, Louisiana, which dealt with engine installation. (Ref 1)

Bayou St John where boats were placed in the water, tested and awaited delivery. (Ref 1)

Higgins plant on St Charles Avenue, New Orleans in 1937. To the left in the photo is an early Wonderboat. (Ref 14)

Bottom view of a Eureka boat showing a single screw, tunnel, flanking rudder and keel. (Ref 29)

Eureka Boat with twin tunnels, 1937. (Ref 14)

A 42ft steel hulled Eureka boat being loaded on a ship to South America. (Ref 14)

A civilian Eureka boat at full speed. (Ref 14)

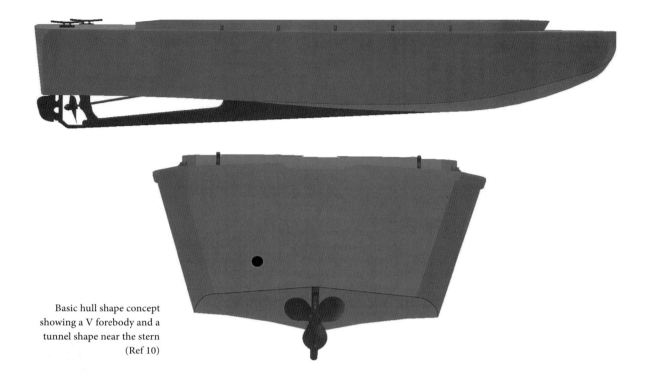

Basic hull shape concept
showing a V forebody and a
tunnel shape near the stern
(Ref 10)

Further research, plus trial and error, increased the speed of the boat to an astounding speed of 20mph. The final product was called the 'Eureka', and was sold to petroleum companies in the United States as well as to those in South America.

There was a problem with wood boats of that time in that when placed in the water they leaked until the planks swelled and sealed the gaps. This was undesirable when a craft that had been out of the water for a period of time was placed in the water and immediately required to be used. Higgins Industries solved this problem by manufacturing a double-bottom boat with a sheet of canvas sandwiched between the two layers. The construction method involved a canvas layer that would cover the underwater hull from the keel to the chine, sealing off the bottom from water leakage.

Sales of the boat increased as its reputation as a practical, shallow draft, workboat became widely known. The US Army Corps of Engineers, the Biological Survey Department, and Coast Guard were all customers.

With the onset of the Second World War, Higgins Industries began selling landing craft based on the Eureka design to the British. At that time landing craft attacks on defended enemy positions were not considered viable by the US military as a result of the experience of the disastrous landings at Gallipoli during the First World War where the British and French forces suffered heavy casualties. However, as the Second World War began to evolve, it would become apparent that landing craft would play a pivotal role.

In 1937 the Navy Fleet Landing Exercise (FLEX) had demonstrated severe difficulties in landing troops on a beach with the existing landing craft. A good landing craft should deliver troops to a beach, rapidly unload them and easily retract through surf, and Andrew Higgins believed that his Eureka boat was far superior to those proposed by the Navy Bureau of Ships. Commander Ralph S McDowell, who was responsible for landing craft under the Convoy and Routing Section of the US Navy, contacted Andrew Higgins and asked him to come to Washington to discuss the employment of the Eureka Boat as a landing craft for military operations. The Eureka was redesigned in 1937 – Higgins was constantly modifying and improving his boats – and four additional Eurekas were ordered in 1938 as there were significant changes since the redesign in 1937. The Navy's specifications for landing craft were also evolving: the boat should be 30ft long, weigh 10,000lbs and carry a load of 5000lbs; there should be room for 18 soldiers and a machine gun, along with armour protection of the gasoline engine and gasoline tank; the speed should be in excess of 10 knots, and be able to land in surf and retract in surf with the use of an anchor.

Typical East Coast fishing boat with pointed bow and flat stern. This was a starting point for the development of landing craft by the US Navy's Bureau of Ships. (Ref 10)

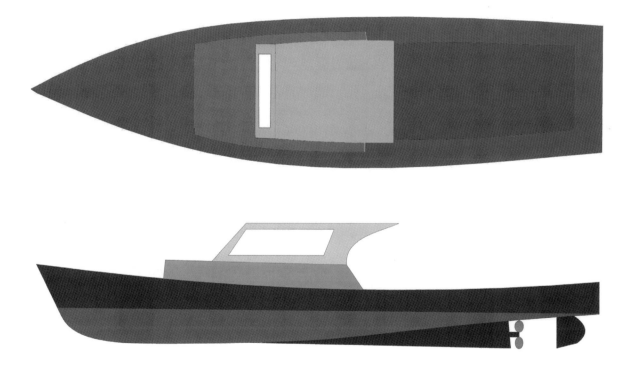

In early 1939 the Navy tested landing craft at the island of Culebra, off the coast of Puerto Rico. The landing craft were modified East Coast fishing boats that had pointed bows for hitting seas head on but flat sterns that made it difficult to retract from a beach. This design was called a Bureau Boat. Many had keels that dug in the sand, also making it difficult to retract the craft.

Typical East Coast US fishing boats. The design of these boats with their pointed bows and flat transoms evolved for the purpose of negotiating deep water and heavy seas. They made poor landing craft. (Ref 10)

A Higgins wooden Eureka with a modified stern to deflect waves to each side appeared to work well and retract without using an anchor. This was a result of the 250hp engine which could pull the craft off the beach easily. The Navy was critical of this high-powered engine since it had increased fuel consumption over other boats that used smaller engines. Higgins argued that the increased horsepower was necessary to pull the craft from the beach.

Another innovation was the addition of a small rudder in front of the propeller which helped in backing off the shore. All boats had a cut-away forefoot (a keel at the after half of the boat only) making it difficult to handle in a crosswind, although it was expected that training of the coxswain would help reduce this handling problem. In August of 1939 the competition for the best landing craft continued, and practice landings by Marines found that the Eureka boat manufactured by Higgins was the most effective in landing and retracting from the beach. The Eureka was declared the winning boat.

Despite the 'not invented here' syndrome of the Navy bureaucracy, in September of 1940 the Eureka was chosen as the landing craft best suited for the Navy and Marines. The Eureka would later evolve into the Landing Craft Personnel Large (LCPL), the Landing Craft Vehicle (LCV), the Landing Craft Personnel Ramp (LCPR), the Landing Craft Vehicle Personnel (LCVP) and the Landing Craft Personnel Nested (LCPN). At first delivery of the Eureka was limited by Hall-Scott gasoline engine production, but the Navy increased supply of these engines by awarding contracts to the Hudson Car Company to manufacture the engine under licence from Hall-Scott. In 1940 the British ordered a longer (36ft) version of the Eureka. The British used a long gangplank that was deployed over the bow so that the troops could exit straight ahead and not have to climb over the gunwales. The British were generally pleased with the performance of the boat as its top speed was 15 knots, 5 knots faster than the equivalent British boat. The British also wanted self-sealing fuel tanks and better protection for the crew. These boats were equipped with the

Hall-Scott gasoline engine. Despite the US Navy's insistence on a 30ft boat, Higgins convinced them that the 36ft type was faster (with the same engine), would carry twice the number of troops and handle better at sea. The Marines pressed the Navy for the new boat, and when in September 1940 it was shown that 36ft boats would fit under the current davits of large ships, it opened the way for an order for 335 of the 36ft Eurekas. Testing of the 36ft boat was successfully completed in October 1940.

The 30ft landing craft designed by the Navy (called a 'Bureau boat'). This design was similar to the typical East Coast fishing boat with the exception of a rounded stern to split waves and a machine gun pit at the bow. The propeller was exposed and could be damaged on beaching. This was a competitor to the Eureka boat. (Ref 10)

BELOW
US Marines carrying out a practice landing using Navy motor launches, which were similar in concept to the Bureau boat. This boat design was unsatisfactory for several reasons: there was a bottleneck at the bow as troops disembarked, which delayed the deployment to the battle area; the coxswain was totally exposed and vulnerable to gunfire; the propeller was easily damaged by the landing ground, which might include rocks; the keel might dig deep into the beach hindering retraction. (Ref 42)

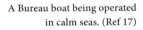

ABOVE
A Bureau boat, the landing craft designed by the Bureau of Ships. It was essentially an East Coast fishing boat with a rounded stern and additional propeller protection. (Ref 17)

A Bureau boat being operated in calm seas. (Ref 17)

An early LCPL (Landing Craft Personnel Large) being lowered for testing at the Higgins plant in New Orleans. (Ref 17)

ABOVE
An early LCPL undergoing trials in New Orleans. (Ref 17)

Coast Guard picket boat (a Eureka boat) being tested on Lake Pontchartrain. This configuration has two gun pits on top of the main cabin. (Ref 15)

A Eureka boat in Manila Bay, Philippine Islands, 1948. Notice the gun pits on top of the main cabin. (Ref 10)

General arrangements of the
36ft Eureka landing craft.
(Ref 10)

The 36ft Eureka was fitted with two forward machine gun pits and the design was adopted as the standard landing craft. The only deficiency of the boat was that the troops got sprayed with water during landings as a result of sea motion and the bow ploughing into the sea. Mass production of the boat began and other manufacturers were contracted to build boats to the Higgins design. There was considerable discussion on whether or not the landing craft should have armour protection. This added weight, reduced speed and limited the capacity of the boat, and the Navy opted not to armour the 36ft Eurekas.

There was also increased interest in installing diesel engines in landing craft. Diesel technology was improving with lighter and higher horsepower models available. There was improved fuel economy with diesel, as well as a significant increase in safety since the fuel is much less volatile than gasoline. The Gray Marine 225hp engine was adopted (GM Diesel 6-71, six-cylinder, 71 cubic inches per cylinder) as the standard engine. There were several different models of the 6-71 and it accounted for 80 per cent of the engines installed on US amphibious ships and craft.

Coxswains on landing craft tended to run the diesel engines at high speed all the time which cut into the expected life of 2000 hours. An adjustment to the engine governor was designed such that two modes could be selected: normal mode and battle mode. The battle mode was the original full speed governed setting. The normal mode was a governed setting of lesser rpm which tended to extend engine life.

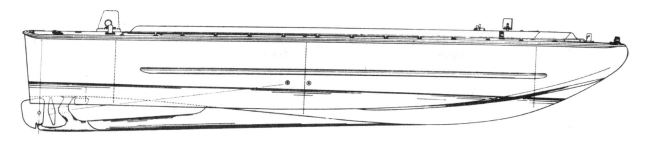

Outboard profile of the 36ft Eureka landing motor boat. (Ref 1)

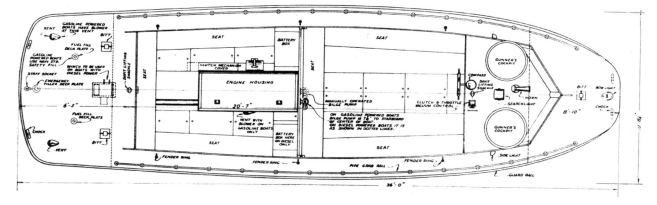

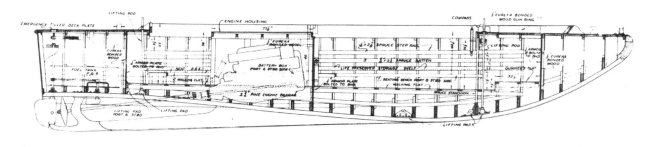

Inboard profile from starboard and plan view of the 36ft Eureka landing motor boat. (Ref 1)

Demonstration of the structural integrity of the Eureka by driving the boat onto a concrete levee on Lake Pontchartrain, Louisiana. (Ref 18)

ABOVE AND BELOW
Two views of the 36ft LCPL showing troops having to jump over the gunwale; this later led to a ramp to facilitate disembarking. (Ref 17; Ref 30)

Soldiers landing from the Eureka boat had to jump over the sides to disembark, which the Marines saw as a significant deficiency because the men became exposed unnecessarily and unloading was not very rapid. Marine personnel had observed Japanese landings in the Far East and brought back photographs of the Diahatsu Type landing craft with a large bow ramp. The ramp appeared to work well and the Marines approached Higgins Industries about installing a large bow ramp on the Eureka. Higgins built three smaller prototype boats with ramps at their own expense. A problem developed with this early design in that the engine was moved to the stern with a V drive, making the boat tail heavy. This caused the rudder and keel to dig into the sand making it difficult to retract. The engine was then moved forward toward amidships to allow a direct drive and better balance of the boat.

The 36ft Eureka was designed with a stern tunnel along with a back-up (flanking) rudder used to aid in retracting from a beach. The craft would spin easily when backed too quickly since it was not equipped with a keel forward of amidships which would tend to stabilize a conventional craft when reversing. Inboard-engined boats are difficult to control going astern since propeller water thrust does not flow past the rudder. The back-up rudder provides some means of controlling the boat while reversing, but it must be performed slowly to maintain control. If the propeller rotates clockwise when travelling forward, then in reverse the stern will move to port. For quick withdrawal from a beach, the coxswain must be ready to accommodate the quick rotation of the hull since the craft will easily yaw around its own length. Consequently, if you approach a dock on the port side, then reversing to cut speed will also bring the stern in and the craft will be parallel to the dock.

Two gun pits were provided at the bow section of the boat on each side of the coxswain position. In 1941 a small personnel ramp approximately 3ft 6in wide was added to the design as a means of offloading troops to the beach. This design was called a LCPR (Landing Craft, Personnel, Ramp).

The origins of the ramp can be traced back to the late 1930s, when the US Navy was struggling with the task of designing a landing craft that would quickly offload troops onto a beach. A war in the Far East was anticipated, which raised the prospect of amphibious landings on several islands. The Marine Corps had a particular interest in landing craft since they were the ones who would have to assault the beach, but the Navy designs derived from East Coast fishing craft had proven unsatisfactory. In 1937 Marine Lieutenant Victor Krulak became involved in the development of landing craft for the Marine Corps. While on duty in China in 1937 he observed a Japanese landing operation against the Chinese. The Japanese landing craft landed troops quickly and backed off the shore without the use of a stern anchor to help pull the boat out to sea. He took photos of the operation (shown on pages 22 and 23) and wrote a report to his superiors on what a landing craft should look like. The Marine generals took the report to the Navy but were rebuffed in favour of more traditional fishing boat designs. The Navy and the Marines did not see eye to eye on amphibious operations – the Navy wanted total control, while

ABOVE LEFT
An LCPL from APA-54 (the attack transport USS *Wayne*) in the South Pacific, 1944. (Ref 18)

ABOVE RIGHT
A troop-laden Eureka landing motor boat with a water cooled 0.30cal machine gun mounted on the foredeck. (Ref 10)

the Marines wanted control over the actual landings. Lt Krulak became the designated expert on landing craft for the Marines and approached Andrew Higgins regarding the ramp design. Higgins immediately saw the value of the concept and manufactured prototype boats with a large bow ramp. This proved very successful in testing, resulting in the Navy eventually adopting the design. Lt Krulak is often credited with driving the development of the ramp.

The Japanese landing craft observed by Krulak was known as the Daihatsu type, which made up about 85 per cent of all Japanese amphibious craft. This design was to be influential in the development of the LCVP (Landing Craft Vehicle Personnel), commonly referred to as the Higgins Boat. The Daihatsu was powered by an 80hp kerosene fuelled motor and had a top speed of 8 knots while the LCVP had a top speed of 12 knots; it weighed 10.5 tons as opposed to the 9 tons of the LCVP. The Daihatsu could carry a load of 10 tons and was constructed of steel. Its bow was catamaran shaped (double bow) which had less drag than the single bow.

Three photos of Japanese landing craft (Daihatsu) taken by Lt Krulak in China in 1937. (Ref 21)

A ramped version of the Eureka was first manufactured in 1942 along the lines of what Lt Krulak suggested. The ramp was 3ft 4in wide with a capacity of 500lbs, the intention being to maintain the low profile of the craft. The Navy then required all Eureka boat manufacturers to change to the bow ramp design with side armour. Of these, the Owens Yacht Company could not make the modification but Chris-Craft could and became the sole provider of the Eureka ramp boat. After much testing the design evolved into the LCVP, which is discussed in detail in Chapter 2.

BELOW LEFT
Steering position on a wrecked Daihatsu. (Ref 22)

BELOW RIGHT
Photo of another type of landing craft, known as Chuhatsu, taken by Lt Krulak. (Ref 21)

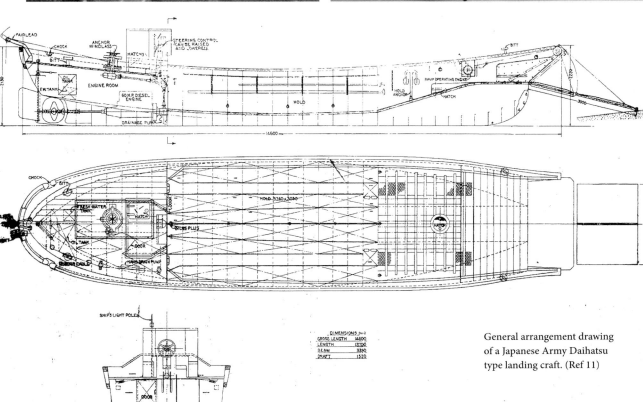

General arrangement drawing of a Japanese Army Daihatsu type landing craft. (Ref 11)

ABOVE LEFT
The ramp used by Japanese landing craft was the inspiration for the Higgins-designed ramp. (Ref 10)

ABOVE RIGHT
The Higgins prototype of the LCVP was a modified 36ft Eureka with the bow cut off to accommodate a ramp similar to the Daihatsu. (Ref 17)

Japanese Army Daihatsu type landing craft at Guadalcanal, 30 November 1942. (Ref 16)

LCPR (Landing Craft Personnel Ramp) with 0.30cal machine guns mounted. (Ref 17)

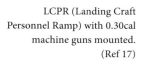

Liberators Courageous..

Brave men . . . massed in landing boats, eager for action, attacking to liberate the oppressed peoples of the world.

Now America strikes with all its might and fury . . . fine fighting forces under capable, courageous officers, with superb equipment.

To make the task easier, to get it done more quickly, American industry must produce more and more . . . all Americans must buy more of the War Bonds that back our fighting forces.

Building the boats shown above in greater quantities than ever before is but a part of the war-time, full-time job of Chris-Craft . . . it's one of our contributions to the cause of Liberty.

For production "Well Done" we proudly fly the Army-Navy "E" at all three Chris-Craft Factories.

★ ★ ★ **CHRIS-CRAFT** ★ ★ ★

CHRIS-CRAFT CORPORATION • 4611 DETROIT ROAD, ALGONAC, MICHIGAN

WORLD'S LARGEST BUILDERS OF MOTOR BOATS

Eureka boats with ramp, in an advertisement
from Chris-Craft. The ramp worked adequately but restricted the offload of troops. Later,
a much larger ramp was added to the final design that allowed for quicker disembarkation. (Ref 10)

CHAPTER 2 The Higgins LCVP Design

When the US entered the Second World War, the Navy was in urgent need of an effective landing craft. Therefore, the bow of the Eureka boat was cut off and a larger, 7ft wide, ramp was fitted to form the basic design of the Landing Craft Vehicle Personnel (LCVP). This allowed a much quicker disembarkation of troops when compared to the smaller ramp of the LCPR. A patent was filed on 8 December 1941 and issued on 15 February 1944 entitled 'Lighter for Mechanized Equipment'. It should be noted that the bow ramp described in the patent had similarities to that of the Daihatsu landing craft. In the patent it is claimed that a bow gate, the full width of the craft, is supported by a transverse hinge and lowered by cables to provide an extension of the cargo deck. This description is identical to that of the Daihatsu of the previous chapter suggesting the existence of what patent law calls 'prior art'. Nevertheless, the patent was granted.

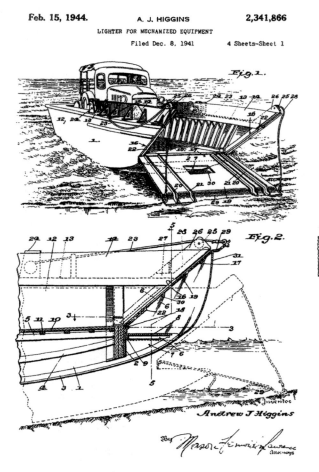

This Higgins patent entitled 'Lighter for Mechanized Equipment' was filed on 8 December 1941 and issued on 15 February 1944. Note the bow ramp is deployed by two cables. (Ref 12)

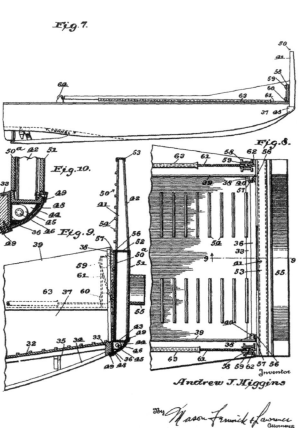

The same US Patent, showing an alternative design for a ramp. (Ref 12)

Watercraft Terminology

Beam:	The maximum width of the hull.
Bow:	The front of the craft.
Bilge:	The lowest inner portion of the craft's hull.
Brightwork:	Polished fittings or varnished woodwork.
Bulkhead:	Upright wall in the hull of a boat.
Chine:	The edge where two planks or two boards meet. Chines can be hard with sharp edges or soft with rounded edges.
Cutwater:	The forward edge of the bow of a boat that cuts through the water.
Deadrise:	The amount of V shape in a hull.
Displacement hull:	A hull that is supported by buoyancy only with no dynamic effects (planing).
Freeboard:	The distance from the waterline of a craft to the gunwale.
Gunwale:	The top of the side of a craft.
Hull speed:	The maximum speed of a displacement hull.
Keel:	The structural beam running along the bottom of a hull.
LOA:	Total length of a craft (Length Over All).
Port:	The left side of a craft when looking forward.
Rake:	An angle
Sheer:	The concave shape of the deck on a boat when looking at the side elevation.
Starboard:	The right side of a boat when looking forward.
Stern:	The rear of the boat.
Stringer:	Long thin pieces of wood used to form the structure of a boat.
Thwart:	A side to side structural support member.
Transom:	The flat board at the stern.
V-Bottom:	A bottom that is shaped as a V.
Waterline:	The level of the water against the hull when the craft is floating in displacement mode.

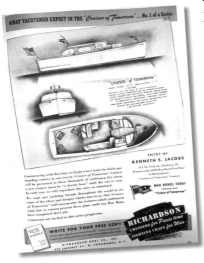

The LCVP was first tested by the Atlantic Fleet Amphibious Force in October 1942, which led shortly afterward to the Navy declaring the LCVP (Landing Craft Vehicle Personnel) to be the standard US landing craft. The LCVP, a descendant of the LCV and LCP, was constructed of wood, primarily of marine mahogany. A steel ramp and side armour were the major metallic components installed on the boat. It was 35ft 9in in length, 10ft 6in wide, with a draft of 3ft 5in fully loaded and a draft of 2ft 2in empty. The cargo compartment was 17ft 3in long, with a maximum width of 7ft 10in and a height of 5ft. The craft weighed 18,500lbs empty and 26,600lbs fully loaded. Maximum speed was 12 knots unloaded and approximately 9 knots fully laden. Early vintage LCVPs that used gasoline engines were later relegated to training, while diesel engine equipped boats were used in frontline operations.

The LCVP typically had four crew members: the Coxswain (captain of the boat), a machinist mate (motor mac) who took care of the engine, and two seamen responsible for deck duties like hoisting the ramp and operating the machine guns. Two gun pits, mounted near the stern, were equipped with 0.30cal machine guns. The bow ramp was hoisted into position by two steel cables connected to an equalizing sheave that was connected to a hand operated winch on the starboard side inside the hull. It took two men to rapidly winch the boat ramp into position prior to sailing. There were several designs of bow ramp depending on manufacturer, as the Navy was not specific on the exact details of various components of the LCVP, allowing some discretion to the supplier. For example, some ramps had a vision slot at the top to observe what was ahead of the boat, others did not; some ramps had parallel bracing while others had X bracing to reinforce the ramp. The ramp provided some armour protection when heading toward shore and extended out approximately 7ft when dropped. Armour protection was added on the port and starboard sides of the cargo compartment in the form of hardened steel sheet 0.2in thick. Since the solid wood bow section of the Eureka had been replaced with a steel ramp, there was a reduction in strength of the bow area. As a result, the gunwales of the boat tended to spread outward because of lack of support of the bow section, sometimes making it difficult to secure the ramp with the dog clamps.

Little attention was paid to the type of infantry unit that would be carried by a landing craft. A platoon was typically 48 men but the boat could carry only 36, so units were divided into assault sections for landing and later reconstituted into the original formation.

Apart from their principal landing role, some LVCPs were equipped with the APEX remote control system and used as drones filled with explosives against beach obstacles. Others were equipped with minesweeping gear or used as control boats. The LCVP was also used extensively to carry cargo to shore, with the loads packaged to facilitate the rapid loading and unloading of supplies in a manner similar to container vessels of today. LCVPs were also used as pusher boats for docking LSTs and as a water taxi ferrying personnel to and from shore.

During the Second World War the LCVP was built by eight manufacturers, with slight differences in production technique. They were Higgins Industries, Chris-Craft, Owens Yachts, Chamberlin Corporation, Dodge Boat and Plane Corporation, Mathews Corporation, Richardson Boat Company, and the 411th Engineer Base Shop Battalion (US Army, Australia). However, all boats essentially conformed to Navy specifications, which reflected the Higgins design with the exception of minor changes in location of deck fittings, etc. Some manufacturers could not duplicate the exact details of the Higgins Industries boats so accommodations were made as long as the basic function of the boat was not compromised.

ABOVE AND PREVIOUS PAGE
Wartime advertisements from various manufacturers of LCVPs.
(Ref 32, Ref 31, Ref.31, Ref 32)

The basic lines and offsets of the hull design are shown on this and the following pages. This drawing is used to form the frame and keel assemblies. The hull is characterized by a full and deep V forebody which tapers to a flat bottom near the middle and a tunnel shape at the stern to protect the propeller during landing and allow for shallow draft. The date on the drawing is 31 March 1945. (Ref 9)

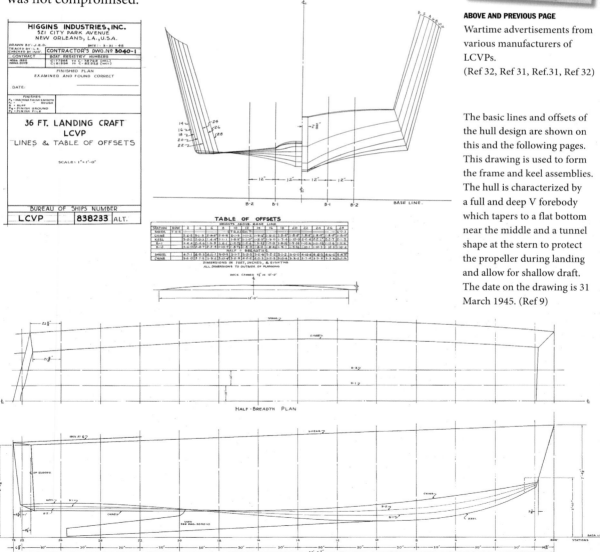

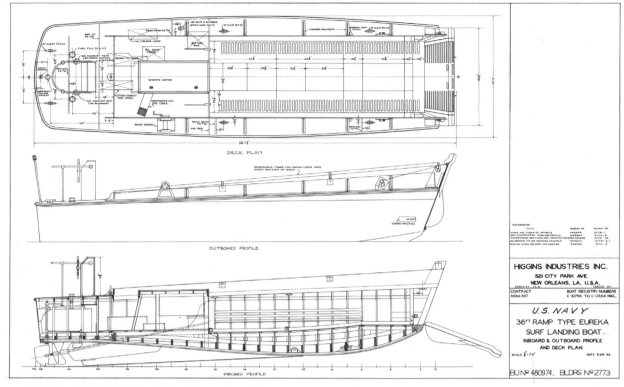

TOP

The builder's drawing shows the rounded or moulded stern characteristic of a boat manufactured by Higgins Industries. Other manufacturers constructed boats using the V stern design shown on the following page which was adopted on later model boats. (Ref 9)

ABOVE

LCV showing exposed helm position on stern and rounded chines. There are no gun pits. (Ref 30)

RIGHT TOP

The LCV was based on the 36ft Eureka boat with a wide ramp in order to transport vehicles. It was unarmed, with the primary duty of delivering cargo to a shore after it was secured by troops landing from the LCP(L), although it could also be used to deliver troops. Later it proved much more useful than the LCP(L), and evolved into the LCVP for carrying both troops and vehicles. (Ref 17)

RIGHT BOTTOM

LCV carrying troops during a training exercise. (Ref 15)

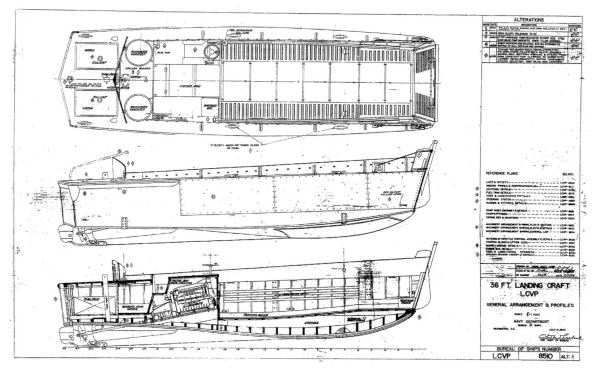

General arrangement and profile plan for the 36ft LCVP dated 9 July 1943. (Ref 9)

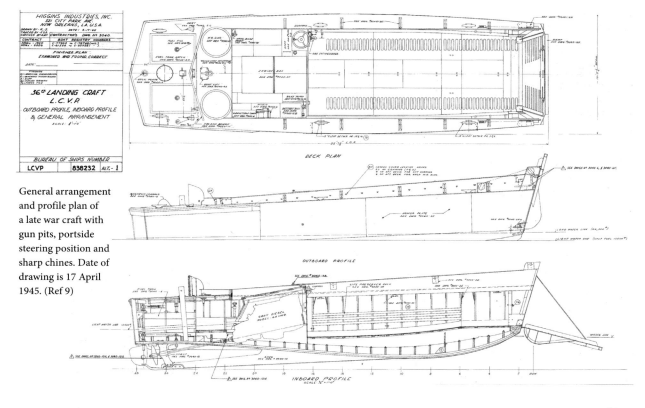

General arrangement
and profile plan of
a late war craft with
gun pits, portside
steering position and
sharp chines. Date of
drawing is 17 April
1945. (Ref 9)

Drawing of engine, transmission and propeller shaft placement for 1945 design. Two fuel tanks were installed near the stern; these were either custom made rectangular tanks or 55 gallon drums adapted to fuel tank use. The Gray Marine diesel engine is shown in the drawing, although early models of the LCVP used the Hall-Scott gasoline engine and the Superior Diesel engine. The strut contains a water lubricated bearing to support the propeller shaft. Just ahead of the strut is the small flanking (auxiliary) rudder used in backing the boat. (Ref 9)

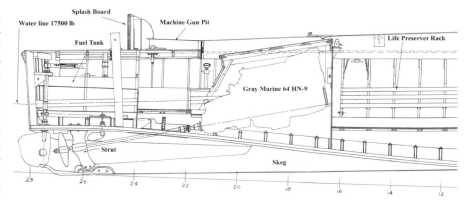

Plan view of the stern and cockpit layout. The helm position is to the left of the engine box (doghouse) and the steering wheel has a telescoping shaft that, in conjunction with a stowed step, could be raised for a clearer view ahead in operations other than combat. The gun rings mounted 0.30cal machine guns on a manually rotating track. Abaft the davit lift fitting is a towing post. The winch is here placed inside the hull, unlike the postwar boats which had the winch outside the coaming. (Ref 9)

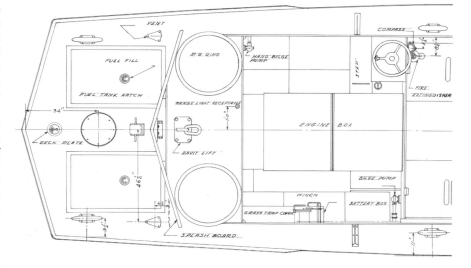

Starboard side view of the middle of the hull. Life preserver racks are on the port side. The cargo deck slopes upward and levels off near the bow ramp. The front davit lift fitting and cable sling fitting is shown at frame 7. (Ref 9)

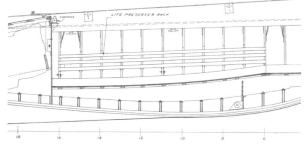

Overhead view of the middle of the hull. The cargo deck has transverse slats in the areas where vehicle tyres travel to maintain grip when loading and leaving the boat. (Ref.9)

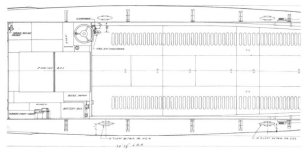

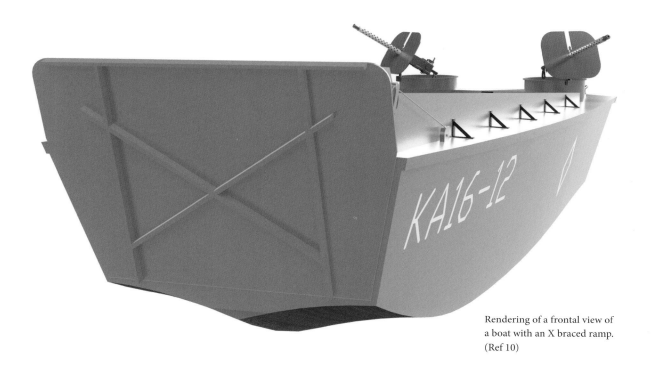

Rendering of a frontal view of a boat with an X braced ramp. (Ref 10)

Rendering of stern view showing the rudder, propeller and gun pits. (Ref 10)

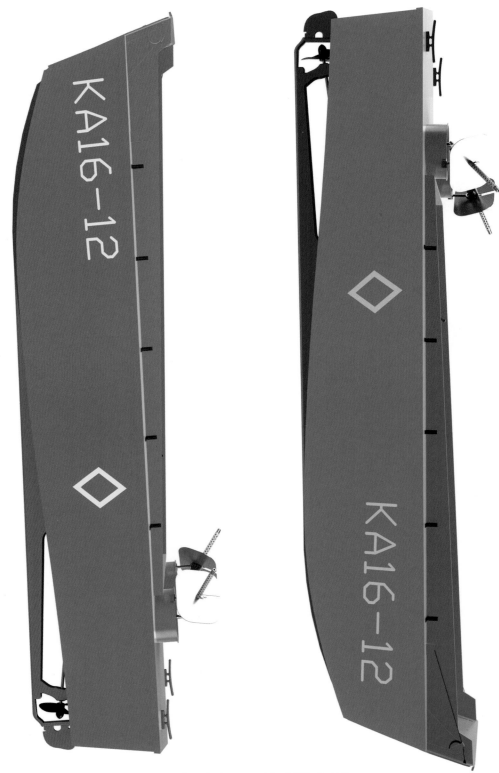

Port and starboard side views of the LCVP. (Ref 10)

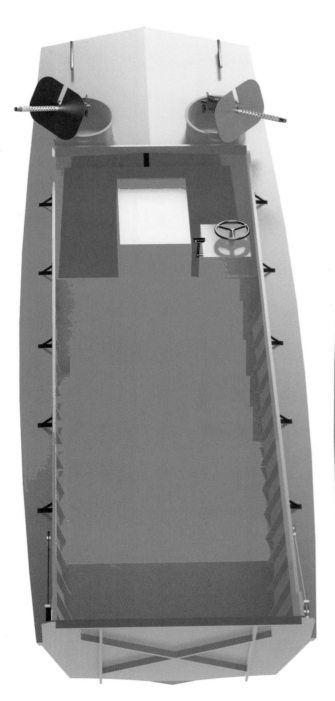

A top view of the LCVP showing the cargo and crew compartment. (Ref 10)

View of the underside. The bow is at the foot of the page with the scuffing bottom shown. Scuffing planks made of oak are placed forward to absorb potential damage from landing on rocky shores. (Ref 10)

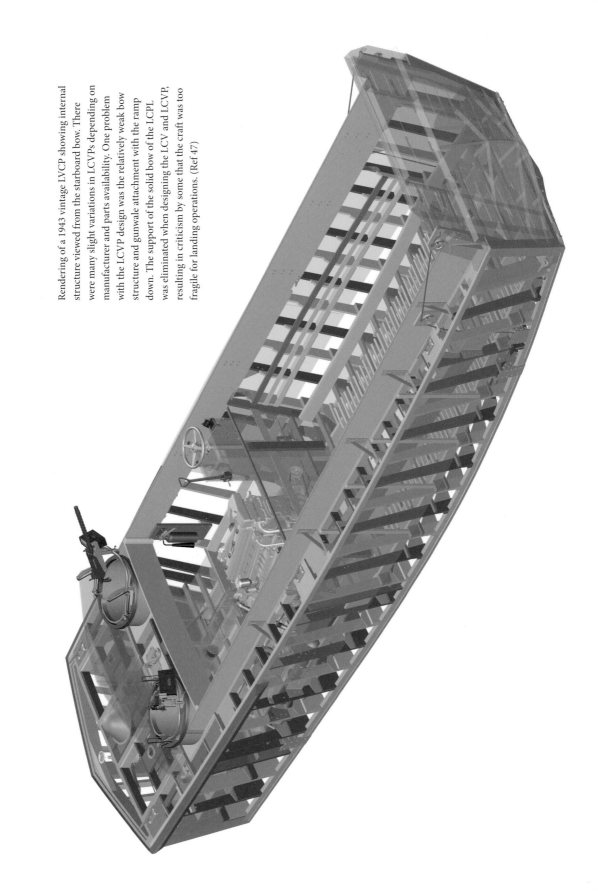

Rendering of a 1943 vintage LVCP showing internal structure viewed from the starboard bow. There were many slight variations in LCVPs depending on manufacturer and parts availability. One problem with the LCVP design was the relatively weak bow structure and gunwale attachment with the ramp down. The support of the solid bow of the LCPL was eliminated when designing the LCV and LCVP, resulting in criticism by some that the craft was too fragile for landing operations. (Ref 47)

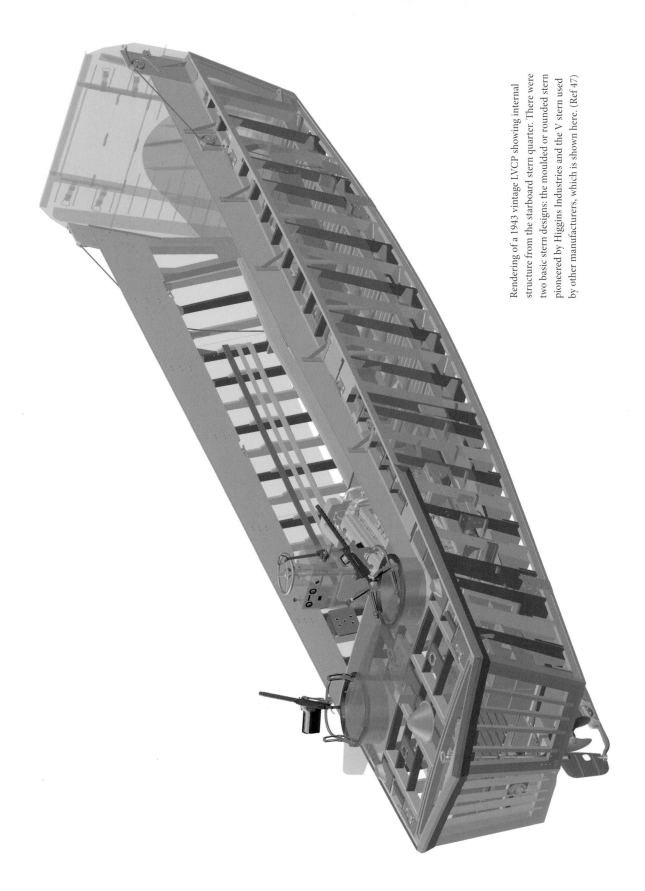

Rendering of a 1943 vintage LVCP showing internal structure from the starboard stern quarter. There were two basic stern designs: the moulded or rounded stern pioneered by Higgins Industries and the V stern used by other manufacturers, which is shown here. (Ref 47)

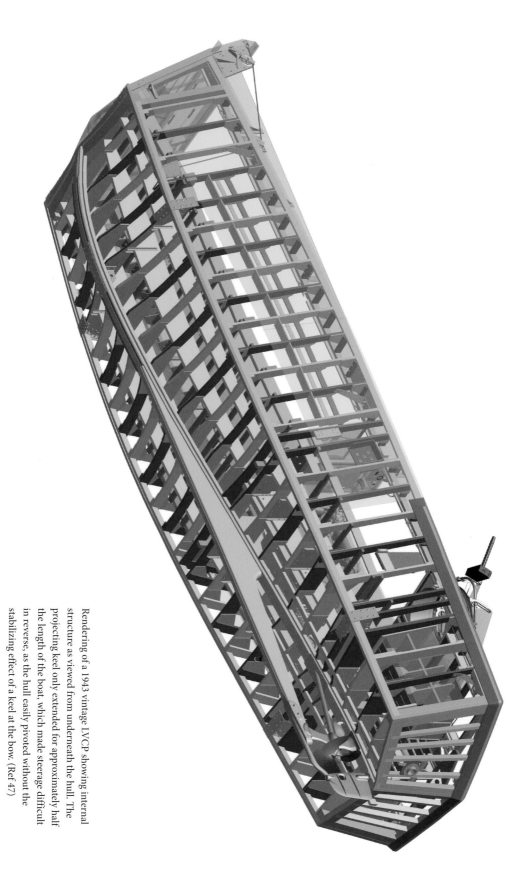

Rendering of a 1943 vintage LVCP showing internal structure as viewed from underneath the hull. The projecting keel only extended for approximately half the length of the boat, which made steerage difficult in reverse, as the hull easily pivoted without the stabilizing effect of a keel at the bow. (Ref 47)

LCVPs embarking troops in England, 1944. (Ref 26)

Jeep and 37mm anti-tank gun being unloaded on a beach with little wave action. (Ref 26)

Examples of the many US Navy camouflage colours from the SHIPS-2 manual published by the US Navy Bureau of Construction and Repair.

Thayer Blue   **Haze Gray**   **Ocean Gray**   **Navy Blue**

A 1943 LCVP with a paint scheme that is similar to Thayer Blue. (Ref 10)

Postage stamps commemorating the LCVP at various battles in the Second World War. (Ref 10)

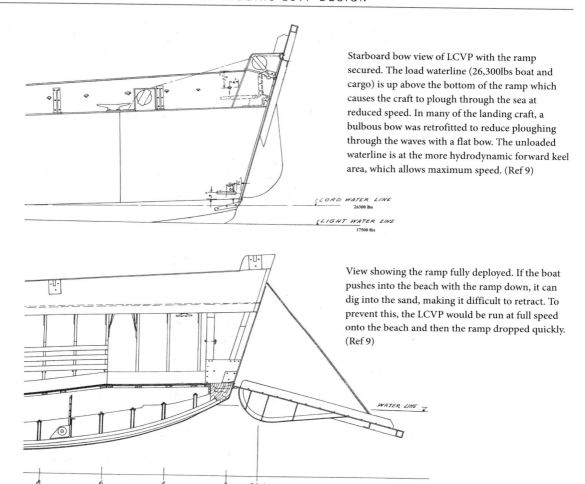

Starboard bow view of LCVP with the ramp secured. The load waterline (26,300lbs boat and cargo) is up above the bottom of the ramp which causes the craft to plough through the sea at reduced speed. In many of the landing craft, a bulbous bow was retrofitted to reduce ploughing through the waves with a flat bow. The unloaded waterline is at the more hydrodynamic forward keel area, which allows maximum speed. (Ref 9)

View showing the ramp fully deployed. If the boat pushes into the beach with the ramp down, it can dig into the sand, making it difficult to retract. To prevent this, the LCVP would be run at full speed onto the beach and then the ramp dropped quickly. (Ref 9)

The expected performance of the LCVP can be examined using classical marine architecture theory of displacement and planing hulls. In displacement mode, a hull is supported entirely by buoyancy forces. In planing mode, the hull is supported by dynamic forces similar to that of water skis. A classical equation based on the Froude Number (Ref 39) used to determine the maximum speed of a hull in displacement mode is:

$$SL = S/(LWL)^{0.5}$$

Where:

S = maximum hull speed in knots (displacement mode)

LWL = waterline length

SL = maximum speed length ratio = 1.34

For the LCVP: LWL = 33.4ft

$$S = 1.34 \times (33.4)^{0.5} = 7.75 \text{ knots}$$

This equation assumes that when the bow wave length of a watercraft reaches the length of the waterline, there is a significant increase in power required to travel faster in displacement mode. This is typically called hull speed in displacement mode.

According to Ref. 34, the maximum speed length ratio SL of 1.34 is a minimum. Higher values can be attained with lighter and narrower hulls and is a function of the displacement–length ratio, (DL) given by the following equation:

$$DL = W/(0.01 \ LWL)^3 \text{ (Ref. 34,36)}$$

Where:

DL = displacement–length ratio

W = weight/2240(long tons)

LWL = waterline length, feet

LCVP hull in displacement mode. Water buoyancy supports the hull as it travels through the water. This mode was often used when cruising, docking or approaching a ship such as an APA transport. The recommended cruising revolutions ranged from 1000 to 1400rpm. Operating at full speed, which is what was often done during combat, would result in reduced engine life. The maximum rpm in normal mode was 1800 while the maximum in combat mode was 2200rpm. (Ref 10)

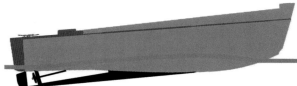

LCVP hull at maximum speed in semi-displacement mode. Coxswains typically piloted the boat at full speed during battle. The bow would lift as a result of dynamic effects (semi-displacement) and the speed would increase if not heavily loaded. (Ref 10)

For the LCVP:

$$DL = (18000/2240)/(0.01 \times 33.4)^3$$
$$DL = 215.7$$

The maximum SL relation from Ref. 34 is given by:
$$SLmax = 8.26/(DL)^{0.311}$$

Where

SLmax = maximum SL the craft can achieve without planing

DL = displacement-length ratio

For the LCVP

SLmax = 1.55

This means the maximum hull speed of the LCVP is $1.55 \times (33.4)^{0.5} = 8.95$ knots. So the maximum hull speed for the LCVP in displacement mode is calculated between 7.75 and 8.95 knots.

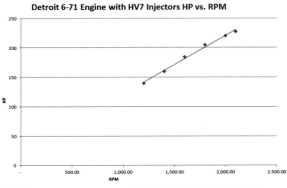

Brake horsepower versus rpm for the Detroit 6-71 with HV7 injectors. (Ref 37)

Another method of calculating the maximum speed of the LCVP is by the following equation often called Wyman's equation:
$$S = C \times (LWL^{0.5}) \times (SHP/(W/1000))^{0.333} \text{ (Ref. 35)}$$

Where:

S = craft speed in knots

C = Wyman Coefficient

LWL= waterline length in feet

BHP = brake horsepower

SHP = Horsepower at the propeller = .95 x BHP assuming 95 per cent efficiency

W = weight of craft

SL = Speed–length ratio

$$C = 0.8 + (0.17 \times SL)$$

$$C = 0.8 + (0.17 \times (1.44)) = 1.0448$$

$$S = 1.0448 \times (33.4^{0.5}) \times (225 \times .95/ (18000/1000))^{0.333} = 13.8 \text{ knots}$$

The previous calculation results in a speed approaching a semi-planing speed for an unloaded LCVP. These calculated maximum boat speeds appear consistent with most reports from veteran coxswains who indicated that the LCVP could rarely travel faster than 9 knots. References 17 and 18 report a maximum speed of 9 knots fully loaded. Maximum speed values are typically 12 knots when unloaded. (Ref. 18).

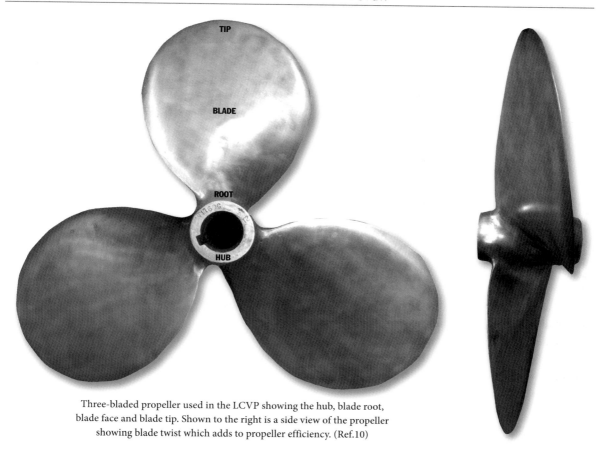

Three-bladed propeller used in the LCVP showing the hub, blade root, blade face and blade tip. Shown to the right is a side view of the propeller showing blade twist which adds to propeller efficiency. (Ref.10)

The propeller used on an LCVP has a 22in diameter and a 20in pitch. Pitch is the distance that the propeller travels in one revolution assuming no slip. The pitch ratio is:

PR = P/D

Where

PR = pitch ratio
P = propeller pitch
D = propeller diameter

The pitch ratio for the LCVP = 20/22 = 0.90 which typically results in propeller efficiencies of around 65 per cent.

Most propellers for the LCVP were right-handed which means the propeller rotates clockwise when in forward gear looking toward the bow. When travelling forward, the propeller tends to push the stern to starboard, although the large steering rudder reduces this effect. When

reversing, the stern moves to port which is more difficult to adjust for since the flanking or backing rudder is much smaller.

The minimum propeller diameter is given by the following equation:

$Dm = 4.07(W \times D)^{0.5}$ (Ref. 34)

Where:

Dm = minimum propeller diameter, inches.
W = beam at the waterline, feet
D = draft, feet

For the LCVP, W = 8ft, D = 3ft, then Dm = 20 inches. The diameter of the LCVP propeller is 22 inches, just barely exceeding the minimum size. A propeller should be greater than the minimum size to assure sufficient thrust at low speed for docking and manoeuvring.

Propeller tip clearance with the hull is a consideration in water craft design. Insufficient tip clearance results in increased vibration and loss of propeller efficiency. The recommended minimum blade tip clearance for a propeller rotating between 300 and 1800rpm is 10 per cent of the propeller diameter. For the LCVP with a 22-inch diameter propeller, the minimum tip clearance is 2.2 inches. In actuality, the clearance was typically 1 inch, which was below that recommended. Since the LCVP must have shallow draft, the clearance and propeller size were kept to a minimum. Good practice on clearance between the rudder and propeller is approximately 15 per cent of the propeller diameter or approximately 3.3 inches for the LCVP. For the LCVP the actual clearance is approximately 4.5 inches.

The angle of the propeller shaft with respect to the waterline results in the most efficiency when the angle is 0. This is impractical since the engine and transmission must sit inside the hull. It is known that shaft angles between 5 and 15 degrees result in no appreciable loss in efficiency. The shaft angle for the LCVP is approximately 13 degrees, which satisfies this criterion.

The propeller shaft size is typically determined by the following equation:

$$D = (321000 \times HP \times SF/(Ys \times RPM))^{0.333} \text{ (Ref. 34)}$$

Where:

D = shaft diameter, inches

HP = shaft horsepower

SF = safety factor, 5-8 for heavy craft

Ys = yield strength in torsional shear of shaft material, PSI

RPM = shaft revolutions per minute

$$D = (321000 \times 225 \times 5/(20000 \times 2100))^{0.333} = 2.05 \text{ in.}$$

The propeller shaft is made of bronze and is 2 inches in diameter, which is sufficient for the horsepower installed in the craft.

Drawing of the propeller shaft location in relation to the underwater hull. As the craft moves forward, a water velocity distribution occurs as shown. The water near the hull is being dragged along at a velocity close to boat speed. This tends to reduce propeller efficiency. Consequently, a large clearance is desirable to increase propeller efficiency. The dichotomy is that the larger the propeller the better, but this decreases propeller clearance which reduces efficiency. Also, a small propeller clearance increases vibration. The clearance on the LCVP is approximately one inch, a compromise in design. (Ref 9)

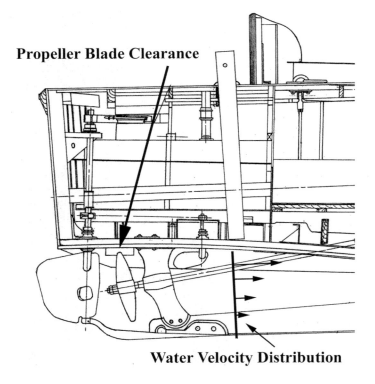

Propeller Blade Clearance

Water Velocity Distribution

Construction

When production of the LCVP was ramped up, it was adapted to assembly line construction. Manufacturing was broken down into various stages, and upon completion of one stage, the hulls were moved on to the next assembly area. Over 23,000 LCVPs were constructed in the Second World War by eight different manufacturers.

It was customary to use wood as a construction material for boats of this size. Wood is compliant, allowing the boat structure to twist and bend with loading from waves and cargo, and wood hulls are also easy to repair. However, a significant disadvantage of wood is that it changes dimension as a function of moisture content. Planked hulls, when taken out of water, dry out and gaps form between the planks. When returned to the water, the boat then leaks until the planks swell and seal off the gaps. Since landing craft may be carried on a large ship for long periods of time in relatively dry conditions, operationally it was impractical to launch such a craft and wait a few days for the hull planks to swell. A landing craft must be used immediately after launch. Higgins Industries solved this with the use of bottom planks covered with canvas and then another layer of planks. This effectively sealed the gaps between planks, allowing the boat to be launched immediately without leakage. Another disadvantage to using wood is that it gouges easily against rocks, so protective measures are required. Steel coping was used on the chines below the waterline and a scuffing bottom of removable external planks was applied to the bottom from the bow to amidships to protect the original bottom planking.

Boatbuilding timber was received from the lumber yard and then stored, having been separated by species. The seasoning was controlled so that boards would reach the appropriate moisture content, resulting in a minimum of internal residual stress. During the 1930s the knowledge of the behaviour of wood was quite extensive. The Forest Products Laboratory was testing wood specimens of various species and reporting on their structural properties such as bending and ultimate strength. It was understood that wood properties were highly variable, depending on many factors. Choosing the proper time to cut a tree for boatbuilding was considered important. Cutting a tree during drier months or in the winter yielded more durable boards since various components of the sap or resin which lead to decay are significantly reduced. Slower growing trees with thinly spaced annular rings yield lumber that is strong and durable.

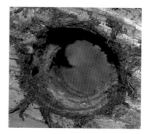
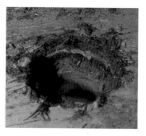

This hole in a Higgins boat reveals the layered wood planks making up the hull. (Ref 10)

BOTTOM LEFT
Timber cross-sections showing classical methods of sawing logs into boards. (Ref 10)

BOTTOM RIGHT
Cross section showing significant parts of a tree. (Ref 10)

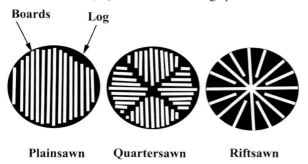

Plainsawn   Quartersawn   Riftsawn

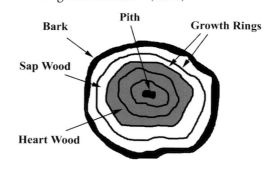

Bark   Pith   Growth Rings

Sap Wood

Heart Wood

By far the most significant parameter affecting the strength and quality of wood is moisture content. Green wood (moisture-laden wood) at 30 per cent or more moisture content may have 1/3 the strength of seasoned or dried wood at 12 per cent moisture content. Wood shrinkage is an important aspect of wood boat design. The maximum amount of shrinkage occurs in the direction tangential to the annular growth rings of the tree. Riftsawn boards shrink less than the quartersawn and plainsawn boards. Distortion of boards from shrinkage can compromise the integrity of a wood hull. Controlling moisture content (seasoning) of the wood was performed to suit the expected use of the particular board. A rule of thumb was that the moisture content of boards should be no more than 16–17 per cent. Moisture content above 20 per cent would lead to decay. Water treatment of the wood was used to remove soluble sap from boards. The board would be placed in a tank of water for a few weeks, then removed and dried naturally. The water tended to draw out soluble resins and sap from the board. Kiln drying is quicker but runs the risk of non-uniform drying and over drying. Kiln temperatures ranged from 100° to 212°F depending on the wood species. Approximately four days of heating was required for 1-inch thick board stock. Hard woods were usually air dried from three to six months and then kiln dried for six to ten days. It was accepted that a moisture content of approximately 15 per cent was best for boat work. Wood that was to be seasoned naturally was placed on racks outside, under shelter from the rain and sun. Spacers were placed between boards, and the long axis of the boards was parallel to the prevailing winds in the area.

The hull form of the LCVP changes from a V bottom at the bow to a tunnel bottom at the stern. Quality stable lumber is required in order to be formed

A wartime view of the City Park Plant assembly line. Boats start construction upside down on support fixtures (foreground) and are eventually turned right side up for installation of engines and related hardware (background). (Ref 26)

THE GUY WHO RELAXES IS HELPING THE AXIS!

to the hull shape without splitting but be sufficiently stable to maintain this shape. There are highly stressed areas on the LCVP near the head log at the bow which require a stable timber that does not warp over time. The head log connections with the gunwale were reinforced with steel gussets, but the stability of the wood that these fixtures are bolted into was very important. The proper seasoning minimized the development of wood checks, cracks and warps. Properly seasoned wood could be applied to the LCVP hull easily and would remain stable throughout the production process. The moisture content for mahogany was typically controlled from 7–14 per cent depending on the part being manufactured. This was aided by kiln drying. Lumber with moisture content below 7 per cent was not used. High moisture content boards were utilized at the bottom of the boat in areas with a high probability of water accumulation such as the bilge area.

Wood for planks was typically air dried out of doors for several months as moisture levels dropped. This was time consuming, hence the usage of kiln dried wood, which required care, as rapid drying could stress and crack the wood. Moisture content was determined by cutting a 1-inch long sample from the wood, placing it in an oven for 24 hours at 212° F and measuring the decrease in weight. The uniformity of moisture was determined by cutting a 1-inch sample and slotting it so that the piece looks like two fingers. If the fingers close together upon drying there is excessive moisture in the wood. If the fingers diverge outward there is more moisture at the surface. If the fingers do not move the wood is uniformly dry.

After assembly, the frame was dipped in a tank of preservative for 5 minutes to reduce deterioration over time. The preservative called Chemi-Seal worked so well that many boat manufacturers continued to use this treatment after the war.

Development of Construction Techniques

Francis W Beasecker was instrumental in the development of construction techniques for the US Army. He had operated a small freighter on the Great Lakes for several years beginning in 1937, and was a marine engine specialist for the Chrysler Corporation in Detroit, Michigan from 1941 to 1942. He applied for a commission in the Engineer Amphibian Command in July 1942 and was commissioned a 2nd Lieutenant in the US Army Corps of Engineers. Initial training was at HQ, Engineer Amphibian Command, Camp Edwards, Massachusetts in August 1942 with a supplemental course of study at Chris-Craft Industries (Algonac, Michigan) which was completed on 10 October 1942. He was assigned to the 411th Engineer Base Shop Battalion, 2nd Brigade, Engineer Amphibious Command in October 1942. He completed another supplemental course of study at Higgins Industries (New Orleans, Louisiana) on 20 November 1942. He then reported to Fort Ord, California, for transport to Cairns, Australia and departed December 1942, arriving in Cairns the following January. He undertook the compilation of an LCVP construction manual under his own initiative. In a memo to HQ, Engineer Amphibian Command (11 October 1942) he wrote:

Francis W Beasecker, 1st Lt, US Army Corps of Engineers. (Ref 2)

39

During the prescribed course of instruction at the Chris-Craft Corporation Boat School, the need for an instruction manual covering the details of hull construction was evident. In addition to my regular duties, I have compiled a rough draft of such a manual which I wish to submit for approval. Engineering data, photographs, detailed drawings, etc were all obtained through the excellent cooperation of Chris-Craft Corporation and the Navy Department. The information contained in this manual was written up and compiled by the writer based on the drawings and photographs made up by Chris-Craft Corporation expressly for this purpose. While the above manual was not authorized, it is being submitted for possible consideration and approval.

Because of the development of this manual and his work on production techniques, Lt Beasecker was awarded a Bronze Star medal on 28 November 1944 with the following citation:

1st Lt (then 2nd Lt) Francis W Beasecker, Corps of Engineers, US Army. For meritorious conduct in the performance of outstanding services rendered in the planning and establishing of a boat construction program at [Cairns and] Port Moresby, New Guinea, from 6 Feb 1943 to 18 Feb 1944. In his capacity as a member of the development section of the Boat Building Command, Lt Beasecker reengineered production lines of partially assembled landing craft to conform with personnel, facilities, and supplies available at that time. With a high degree of professional skill attained after months of exhaustive study in boatbuilding techniques, he developed a training program in methods of landing craft production, which proved to be of invaluable service. At a time when the war effort was hampered by a critical shortage of landing craft, Lt Beasecker, by his keen technical knowledge, sound judgment, and capable leadership, contributed materially to the success of military operations in the South West Pacific.

Several of the photos in this chapter were taken from the manual developed by Lt Beasecker.

Choosing the appropriate timber for manufacturing the LCVP came from years of experience at Higgins Industries. Philippine mahogany (also called tangile, red luan, white luan, or tiaong) was used in the construction of the LCVP. Tropical cedar comes in many varieties but is often referred to as Philippine mahogany as it looks like real mahogany. The dark red variety is hard, decay resistant and has a high ultimate strength. The trees yield large clear boards without knots and checks. Knots and checks can crack over time and compromise the seaworthiness of the hull.

Typically, boat construction started by laying out the frames, bulkheads and keel with the boat upside down on a form or temporary support structure. Then the boat would be righted to accept the engine, fuel tanks and other heavy hardware. Many parts were prefabricated for quick assembly on the floor. At this early stage of construction considerable skill was required from the workmen to obtain the proper dimensions and fit of the frames and keel. An improper fit would result in future problems with installing other parts further down the production line.

The form that supports the keel and frames in the first phase of construction. The hull is upside down at this stage. (Ref 2).

The head log (first bow frame) bolted to the first support on the construction form. The vertical bow posts are then attached to the head log. (Ref 2)

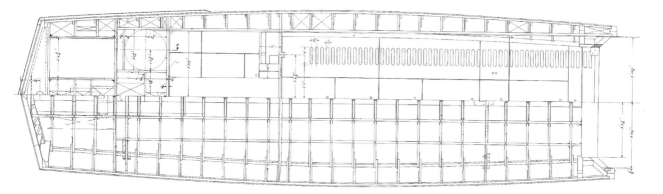

HALF-HULL FRAMING, HALF-DECK PLAN
(DECK REMOVED)

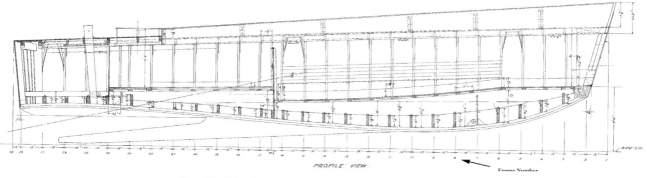

PROFILE VIEW

Frame Number

Profile and half-hull framing plan; drawing dated 13 February 1945. (Ref 9)

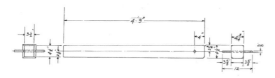

Tow Post

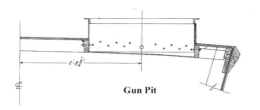

Gun Pit

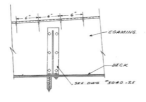

COAMING BRKT. ASSEMBLY
SCALE: 1½" = 1'-0"

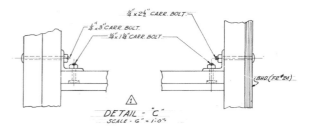

DETAIL - "C"
SCALE - 6" = 1'-0"

Drawings of sub-assemblies in
the LCVP. (Ref 9)

HATCH TRIM
SCALE: 3" = 1'-0"

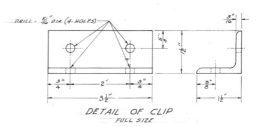

DETAIL OF CLIP
FULL SIZE

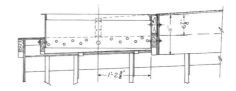

Gun Pit

ABOVE LEFT
Head log and frames clamped to the form. (Ref 2)

LEFT
Starboard view of frames, head log and keel attached to the hull form. (Ref 2)

ABOVE
Bottom tunnel framing at the stern. (Ref 2)

Higgins Industries developed assembly-line techniques in the manufacture of the LCVP very much like Henry Ford developed automobile production lines. At certain stages in production, prefabricated parts of the hull would be assembled and the hull would move to the next stage of production.

The typical sequence of construction was as follows.

The first frame or head log is clamped to the form as well as rib sections along the hull. The rib sections or frames are numbered from 1 to 27 (see previous drawing of the hull assembly). The ribs are set in the form with the designated front side facing forward. The head log is placed in the form and screwed against a guide plate for alignment. The central wood strip (inner keel or apron) is also clamped and prepared for fastening. The keel is then fastened to the apron (inner keel) and frame using galvanized or brass carriage bolts and brass screws.

The transom frames are installed using carriage bolts and bolted to a transom timber which was attached to frame number 27. The tunnel toward the stern is apparent as the stringers and spacer boards are installed. The frames are notched to receive stringers and other frame members. Typically brass screws or galvanized steel nails are used to attach the stringers to the hull.

TOP LEFT
Side framing. (Ref 2)

TOP RIGHT AND BELOW
Transom (stern) framing with hull inverted in photo, and right way up in rendering. (Ref 2, Ref 10)

BOTTOM LEFT
Plywood transom panel installed. (Ref 2)

BOTTOM RIGHT
Inner planking beginning to be installed. (Ref 2)

TOP LEFT
Keel plates being installed.
(Ref 2)

TOP RIGHT
Canvas is glued to inner
planking to seal the gaps
between planks. (Ref 2)

BOTTOM LEFT
The completed bottom of one
boat. (Ref 2)

BOTTOM RIGHT
The completed plywood side.
(Ref 2)

The transom panel that is constructed of a single piece of plywood is fastened to the transom ribs using brass screws. The plywood is formed and cut prior to assembly. The material is plywood but was often referred to as Weldwood which is a product of the United States Plywood Corporation. Then the first layer of the planking skin is secured by common nails.

The inner planking is covered with marine glue and canvas is placed over the planking, draped over the chine and secured with staples. This forms a water-tight barrier sealing the gaps between planks. This boat can be used immediately without having to wait for the wood to swell and seal off leaks. The outer planking or sheathing is then installed. Screws are angled toward the keel to pull the planks toward the keel for a tight fit.

TOP LEFT
Template used to facilitate
accurate drilling of the tunnel
that accepts the stuffing box
fitting and propeller shaft.
(Ref 2)

TOP RIGHT
Alignment of skeg with
propeller shaft pilot hole.
(Ref 2)

BOTTOM LEFT
The bearing in the strut (shaft
bracket) is aligned with the
stuffing box fitting. (Ref 2)

BOTTOM RIGHT
Skeg being jacked into
position and attached to the
hull. (Ref 2)

A hole is drilled into the hull at a location 66.5 inches from the stern to accept the propeller shaft stuffing box mounting plate. A fixture was mounted to serve as a guide for the propeller shaft pilot hole. A pilot hole is drilled so that a plumb line can be used to align the location of the strut (propeller shaft bracket) and skeg assembly.

The skeg and strut are aligned and attached to the hull. This allows the propeller shaft to align with the engine transmission output shaft which reduces vibratory loading of the coupling. This is a critical operation, since the performance of the boat will be degraded with improper alignment. The propeller shaft strut bearing is installed along with the rudder and backing rudder assembly. The tunnel plate, a thin piece of sheet metal, is installed just above the rudder to protect the hull from rocks and debris kicked up by the propeller.

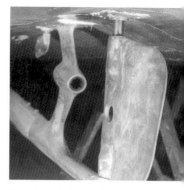

Shaft tunnel plate and strut installed. (Ref 2)

A close-up of the grooves in the strut bearing. These bearings are typically lubricated by water flowing through the grooves as a result of propeller thrust or forward movement of the boat. (Ref 10)

The propeller and shaft have been installed through the strut bearing. (Ref 10)

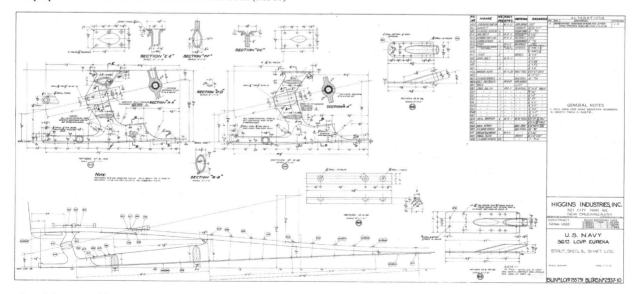

Detail drawings of the strut, skeg and propeller shaft design for a 1944 vintage boat. (Ref 26)

A forward lifting lug between frames numbered 10 and 11 and two stern lifting lugs between frames 21 and 22 are installed using large brass carriage bolts (5/8in x 3.5in) to secure the lugs to the hull. A three-point cable sling is attached to the lugs when launching the boat using a boom crane.

In order to protect the hull during repeated landings, a scuffing bottom, or false bottom, is applied to the hull from the bow to about amidships. Oak planks are attached using brass bolts bolted through the hull. From three to six planks on each side of the keel are installed, depending on the manufacturer. The 3-inch keel strip used to protect the keel during beaching is made of brass or galvanized steel, depending on the manufacturer. Scuffing bottom planks are replaced periodically when worn and no longer protecting the hull.

BELOW LEFT
Forward lifting lug. (Ref 2)

BELOW RIGHT
Starboard stern lifting lug. (Ref 2)

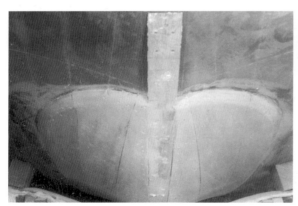

ABOVE LEFT
Scuffing bottom planks in the bow area. (Ref 2)

ABOVE RIGHT
Scuffing plank being installed near the keel. (Ref 10)

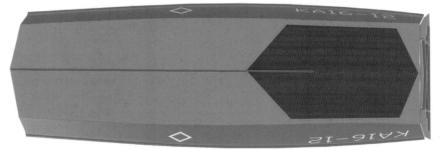

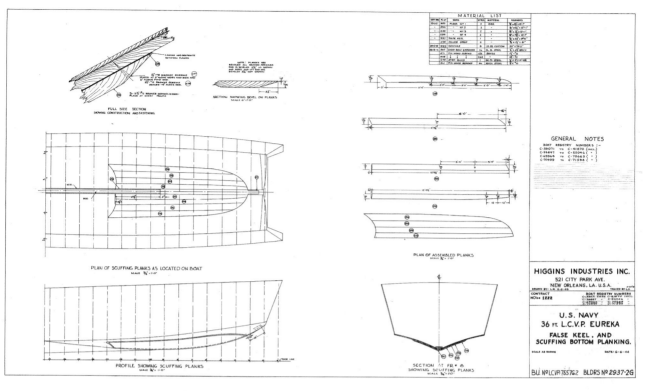

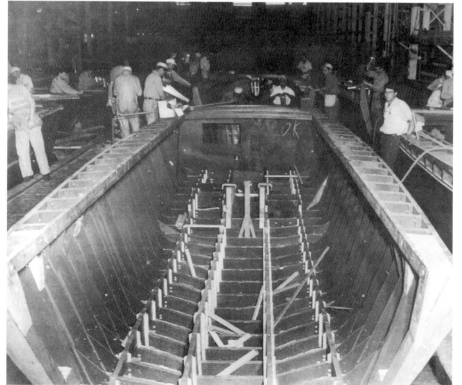

ABOVE

Scuffing bottom planking layout dated 6 June 1944. This layout is slightly different from that of the 1943 boat depicted on the previous page. (Ref 26)

View of hull after being turned upright showing framing completed. Installation of decking stringers and supports will now commence. (Ref 9)

TOP LEFT
Cargo deck stringers installed. (Ref 2)

TOP RIGHT
Engine mounts. (Ref 2)

ABOVE LEFT
Engine mount. (Ref 2)

ABOVE RIGHT
Manoeuvring rudder control lever. (Ref 2)

The cargo deck stringers are attached to the frame sections using angle irons and carriage bolts. The deck must support 36 troops or a jeep and small artillery piece. The engine mounts are between frames 16 and 22. Steel gussets are part of the engine mount; the engine weighs approximately 2900lbs.

The engine is at such an angle to accommodate the alignment with the propeller shaft. Misalignment must be minimized to accommodate the propeller shaft coupling and the transmission shaft coupling. The manoeuvring or backing rudder (sometimes called flanking rudder) assembly is installed between frames 25 and 26. A stuffing box is provided to seal the manoeuvring rudder shaft from the ocean water. The manoeuvring rudder aids in reverse operations of the craft.

The Gray Marine engine weighs approximately 2900lbs, not including the transmission, requiring a hoist and three or four workers to lift, set and align the engine on the engine mounts. It is critical to make sure that the transmission propeller shaft coupling is aligned with the propeller shaft to reduce vibration and assure a proper seal in the stuffing box that prevents water leakage into the engine compartment. Once the engine is secured to the mounts, the throttle linkage and gear shift lever rod are connected to the control handle which is on the starboard side of the wheel box. An electric cable is connected to the starter and control wiring to the starter solenoid. The workers in the

foreground of the illustration above are preparing to install cooling system fittings once the engine is secured to the engine mounts. Behind the worker in the left foreground, is the cooling system strainer used to filter out sand that is ingested when landing. The valve he is holding controls water flow from the suction fitting under the hull to the heat exchanger on the engine.

The fuel tank mounting boards are secured to frames 25, 26 and 27. This is for the rectangular fuel tank design. Cylindrical fuel tanks in the shape of 55 gallon drums were also used and sit on a semi-circular support.

Steering quadrant.
(Ref 10)

BELOW
Steering quadrant with cables attached. The steering quadrant is clamped to the rudder shaft and acts as the method of transferring the force in the steel cables to a torque to move the rudder. (Ref 10)

RIGHT
Rudder and shaft. (Ref 2)

ABOVE LEFT
Steering quadrant, rudder post and lever arm on a Higgins manufactured boat. (Ref 2)

ABOVE RIGHT
Push rod linkage connected to manoeuvring rudder on a non-Higgins built boat. (Ref 10)

The steering rudder shaft is attached to a steering quadrant which is connected to the steering cables. The steering quadrant clamps to the top of the steering rudder shaft. The steering cables run alongside the hull via pulleys and are wrapped around the steering wheel shaft. The steering rudder and flanking rudder are connected by a linkage push rod. It should be noted that stringer spacing at the transom varied depending on the manufacturer.

The hole in the rudder is to facilitate the removal of the propeller shaft when the rudder has been installed. At right full rudder, the propeller shaft can fit through the hole and be removed without having to remove the rudder assembly. Propeller shafts can become bent or worn, so this feature reduces maintenance related time.

LEFT

View of the aft bulkhead and access hatch into the stern compartment, which housed the steering gear, rudder shaft support and fuel tanks. (Ref 2)

BELOW

The aft deck and circular forms for the gun pits. This deck was well sealed to prevent leakage while operating in heavy seas. (Ref 2)

TOP LEFT

Frame extension and gussets that support the deck and the coaming boards. (Ref 2)

TOP RIGHT

Installation of filler blocks used to maintain spacing of the boards that support the deck. (Ref 2)

ABOVE LEFT

Filler blocks are installed at the bow section. (Ref 2)

ABOVE RIGHT

Transom filler block installed. It should be noted that the rounded transom area is characteristic of the Higgins Industries boat. Boats by other manufacturers were not rounded, as it was easier to manufacture a right-angle corner of the transom. Later versions of the Higgins Industries boats did not have this rounded feature. (Ref 2)

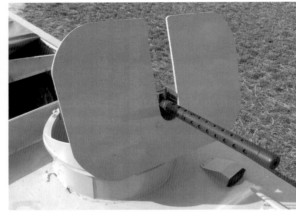

TOP LEFT
Close-up of the gun ring hole in the deck, which conforms to the circular deck structure underneath, ready to accept the gun ring housing. (Ref 2).

TOP RIGHT
Gun pit housings installed. (Ref 2)

ABOVE LEFT
Gun trolley, gun mount, gun shield and back rest installed. (Ref 10)

ABOVE RIGHT
Frontal armour shield for the machine gun. (Ref 10)

RIGHT
M40 machine gun cradle and Browning ammo box. (Ref 10)

0.30 Inch Mount, Mark 21
Cal. .30 BAM Gun 1919-A4
Right Side View

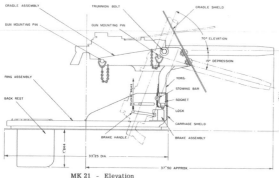

MK 21 - Elevation

TOP LEFT

Gun pit position on an LCVP with 0.30cal machine guns. This is the Mark 21 concentric ring mount. These provided covering fire when withdrawing from a beach but were difficult to use in an assault as it was dangerous to shoot over the heads of the troops in the cargo compartment. (Ref 26).

TOP RIGHT

View of the gun position. (Ref 10)

BOTTOM LEFT

M41 gun mount on an LCVP. (Ref 26)

ABOVE LEFT

Mark 21 Navy 0.30cal machine gun mount used on many LCVPs. The M40 machine gun cradle secured the machine gun to the mount, allowing for manual elevation and traverse by the gunner. The US Army attempted to use this mount on the ¼-ton Jeep but did not adopt it as standard equipment in the Second World War. (Ref 45)

ABOVE RIGHT

M41 machine gun mount also used on the LCVP. (Ref 45)

TOP LEFT
Coaming boards installed. (Ref 2)

TOP RIGHT
Ramp sheave which carries the cable that hoists or lowers the ramp. There are additional sheaves installed in the bilge along with an equalizing sheave that is connected by cable to the winch. The winch on wartime boats was inboard of the coaming; post-war boats had the winch and cable installed outside the coaming. (Ref 2)

ABOVE LEFT
The winch is mounted on a platform attached to the starboard inboard side of the hull. (Ref 2)

ABOVE RIGHT
Winch installation on a 1943 vintage LCVP. Fittings varied over the war years and varied between manufacturers. The large handle in the foreground controls a brake that aids in lowering the ramp. (Ref 10)

RIGHT
Installation of a sealing strip between the hull and the ramp to prevent water entry while under way. (Ref.2)

ABOVE LEFT

Bilge pump which was driven by a belt (left in photo) and the manual pump to the right. (Ref 2)

ABOVE RIGHT

The engine installation showing routing of the exhaust system. The exhaust pipe for the Gray Marine engine was to the port side of the keel unlike that of the early Eureka boats. (Ref 2)

LEFT

Area below the steering wheel box with the clutch linkage rod in the middle of the photo. (Ref 2)

BOTTOM

Typical stuffing box propeller shaft seal fitting. The bolts compress the lubricated stuffing material to form a seal against the propeller shaft to prevent water entry into the hull. (Ref 10)

BELOW

Propeller shaft stuffing box and fairing. This seals the propeller shaft from water entry into the hull. (Ref 10)

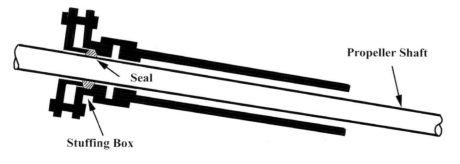

Seal

Propeller Shaft

Stuffing Box

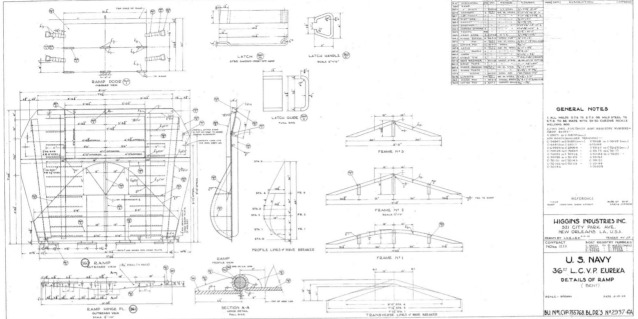

ABOVE

Drawings of bent ramp and bulbous bow wave breaker, dated 19 May 1944. (Ref.9)

RIGHT

Installation of the ramp and bulbous bow feature used to deflect waves. Boats that did not have the bulbous bow ('wave breaker') had ramps that were essentially flat. (Ref 2)

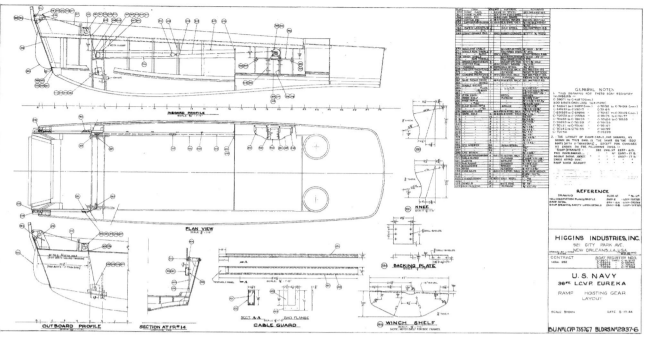

Ramp hoist design showing winch, cables and equalizer pulley box.
(Ref.9)

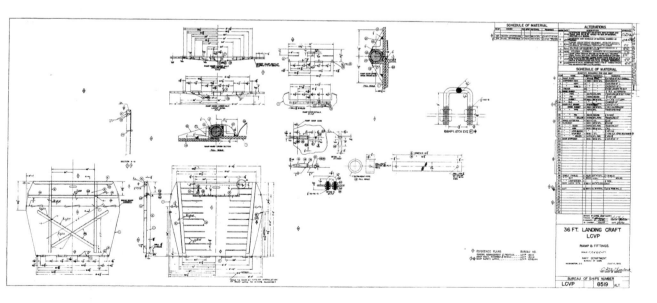

Straight ramp design and associated fittings. (Ref 9)

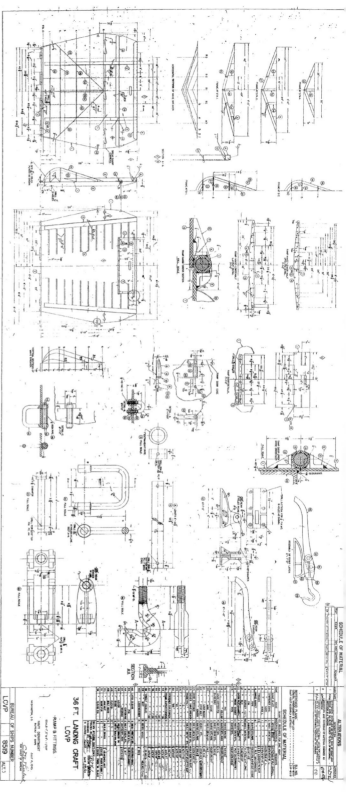

TOP

Registry number inscribed in the keel.
This is a 1943 boat registry number.
(Ref 10)

ABOVE

Typical watercraft identification plate
used by Higgins Industries.
(Ref 13)

RIGHT

Fittings associated with ramp
operation including shackles and ramp
locking clamps (dogs). This is an early
ramp with contoured wave breaker.
(Ref 9)

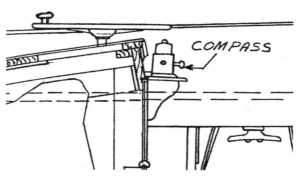

FAR LEFT

Mark 2 Navy compass mounted against the front of the wheel box on an LCVP. (Ref 10)

LEFT

Drawing of the compass mount in front of the wheel box. (Ref 10)

The Mark 2 Navy Compass is a standard liquid filled magnetic compass used in many landing craft. The liquid damps oscillations of the indicator needle. The compass was a necessity in that smoke or fog often obscured the landing area, and the only means of navigation was the compass.

A more advanced compass system is the gyro flux gate compass. The flux gate is a sensor using two or more wire coils wrapped around a magnetic material which detects the earth's magnetic field and transmits a signal through an amplifier to the remote compass indicator. It tends to be more accurate since the sensor or sending unit can be placed in any area of the hull, away from metallic components that can distort the reading. A gyroscope stabilizes the sensor. A remote compass indicator is placed near the wheel box for easy viewing by the coxswain. The system is powered by the main batteries on board the LCVP. This system was also used on aircraft.

ABOVE

Remote compass indicator or repeater. (Ref 10)

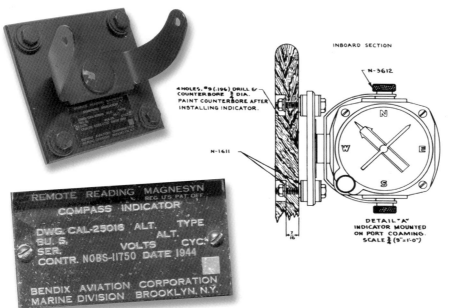

FAR LEFT

Remote compass indicator mount. (Ref 10)

LEFT

Mounting installation drawing for the remote compass indicator. This was typically mounted on the coaming board next to the coxswain. (Ref 10)

BOTTOM

Plaque showing data on the remote compass indicator. (Ref 10)

Drawing showing the installation of the Gyro Flux Gate compass system in an LCVP. The sensor is located at the stern away from metal hardware to minimize distortion or attenuation of the earth's magnetic field. (Ref 10)

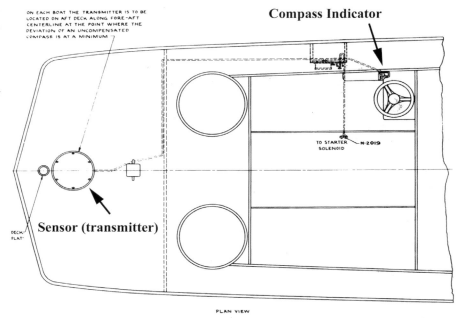

Compass Indicator

ON EACH BOAT THE TRANSMITTER IS TO BE LOCATED ON AFT DECK ALONG FORE-AFT CENTERLINE AT THE POINT WHERE THE DEVIATION OF AN UNCOMPENSATED COMPASS IS AT A MINIMUM

TO STARTER SOLENOID   N-2019

Sensor (transmitter)

DECK PLATE

PLAN VIEW

AFT ◄─── ───► FWD

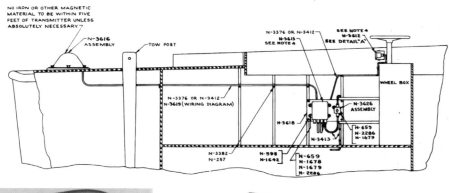

NO IRON OR OTHER MAGNETIC MATERIAL TO BE WITHIN FIVE FEET OF TRANSMITTER UNLESS ABSOLUTELY NECESSARY

BELOW LEFT
Gyro Flux Gate Transmitter (sensor). (Ref 10)

BELOW RIGHT
Amplifier. (Ref 10)

In 1943 the 411th Engineer Base Shop Battalion, US Army was assigned to Cairns, Australia with the mission to construct an assembly plant and manufacture LCVPs. A 450ft long building was adapted for an assembly line for LCVPs at Cairns harbour. Lt Frank W Beasecker of Company B was charged with setting up the production line and the procedure for manufacturing boats. Wood for the LCVPs was supplied by Cairns Timber Mill in Cairns. Engines, transmissions, propellers and other hardware were imported from the United States. Production increased to a peak of seven boats per day using the techniques espoused by Lt Beasecker based on his experience at the Higgins plant in Louisiana and the Chris-Craft plant in Michigan. The Gray Marine engine was the only power plant installed in the LCVPs at this facility. As demand for LCVPs decreased around 1944, the plant began manufacturing larger LCMs (Landing Craft Mechanized).

BELOW
Photograph of a nearly completed LCVP ready for launching. Lt Beasecker is at the left in the sun helmet directing the construction operation. The boat is ready to be hoisted on the monorail to be loaded on the launching cradle. Ref 2)

LEFT
Newly completed LCVPs with the identification numbers added, which is the last step in production. (Ref 27)

RIGHT
Hull 867 being fuelled and readied for launching on the mobile cradle. This is a rare view of the frame system that supports the tarpaulin that covers the boat aboard ship to reduce rain water accumulation in the boat. (Ref 27)

BELOW
Production line with the sides and bottom of boats completed. (Ref 27)

A more advanced stage of completion showing coaming boards, propeller shaft, rudder and ramp added. (Ref 27)

Gray diesel engines ready for installation in the shop area. Shown on each engine is the heat exchanger, a marine adaptation to the GM 6-71 diesel engine. (Ref 27)

ABOVE

Transporter used to deliver LCVPs to the user, typically a shipyard or Navy base on the coast. This truck is being loaded in the Detroit area. Writing at the port bow suggests that this LCVP is destined to be loaded on *LST-819* (Landing Ship Tank 819), USS *Hampshire County* that was launched on 21 October 1944 in Evansville, Indiana. A cradle has been placed on the flat bed trailer for hauling to the destination. (Ref 9)

LEFT

What appears to be a prototype of a landing craft. Higgins Industries was constantly experimenting with different hull designs. (Ref 9)

The Power Plant

CHAPTER 4

The LCVP was designed to utilize a single engine and single propeller shaft. Although some civilian boats of the same length were designed with twin engines and propeller shafts, having dual propulsion on the LCVP would have been impractical due to space restrictions. The civilian boats had a superstructure for the bridge and cabins, while the LCVP did not, which limited the space for propulsion systems. There were four engine models used in the LCVP – the Hall-Scott gasoline engine, the Kermath gasoline engine, the Superior Diesel engine and the Gray Marine diesel engine. The Gray Marine diesel was by far the most common power plant used in the LCVP.

The Hall-Scott Engine Company

The Hall-Scott 250hp Invader 168 gasoline fuelled engine was used in the LCPLs and early LCVPs. It was a six-cylinder 997.8 cubic inch displacement engine with maximum rpm of 2100. The engine used SAE 20 to 40 weight oil depending on environmental conditions. Engine operating temperature was approximately 140° F.

Compared to early diesel engines, gasoline engines had a high power to weight ratio, making them desirable for high speed boats and landing craft. The maximum engine speed was governed at 2100rpm with a cruising speed of

RIGHT
Carburettor side of the Hall-Scott Invader 168 showing two carburettors installed. (Ref 14)

BELOW RIGHT
Exhaust manifold side of the Hall-Scott Invader 168 showing the starter and spark plug wiring. (Ref 48)

BELOW
Training of Navy personnel on the Hall-Scott engine at Higgins Industries, New Orleans, Louisiana. The machinist mate ('motor mac') would attend this course as he was responsible for operation of the engine. (Ref 15)

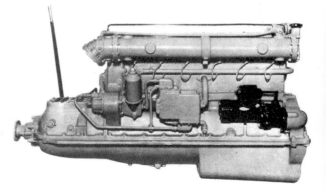

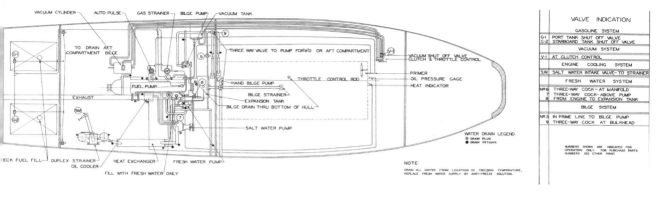

VALVE INDICATION		
GASOLINE SYSTEM		
G-1	PORT TANK SHUT OFF VALVE	
G-2	STARBOARD TANK SHUT OFF VALVE	
VACUUM SYSTEM		
V-1	AT CLUTCH CONTROL	
ENGINE COOLING SYSTEM		
S.W.	SALT WATER INTAKE VALVE - TO STRAINER	
FRESH WATER SYSTEM		
Nº6	THREE-WAY COCK - AT MANIFOLD	
7	THREE-WAY COCK - ABOVE PUMP	
8	FROM ENGINE TO EXPANSION TANK	
BILGE SYSTEM		
Nº5	IN PRIME LINE TO BILGE PUMP	
9	THREE-WAY COCK AT BULKHEAD	

1000-1400rpm. The engine weight was 1950lbs. At the beginning of the Second World War, the Hall-Scott Company could not keep up with engine demand. At that time, official US policy favoured having two or more suppliers for any single piece of equipment designated for the war effort. Consequently, the US Government enlisted the help of the Hudson Motor Car Company to manufacture engines under licence granted by Hall-Scott. The Hudson-manufactured engine had slightly more power than the original Hall-Scott Invader. It also had exhaust manifolds with 'Hudson' cast into the metal in a prominent position.

At the beginning of the war, the transition from gasoline engines to diesels was underway. The power to weight ratio of diesel engines was improving, and diesels were more fuel efficient so less refuelling was required, a plus for a vessel in combat. Furthermore, as pointed out earlier, gasoline is much more volatile than diesel fuel, requiring a bilge ventilation system to prevent the heavier-than-air gasoline vapours from accumulating in the bilge and becoming ignited. Most of these gasoline engine powered boats were used for training purposes only. See Appendices A & B for detailed drawings of the Hall-Scott installation.

Hall-Scott engine layout for the Eureka. Since the helm was at the front of the boat, a vacuum control system was used to operate the throttle and engine clutch. A large thrust vacuum cylinder located to the left rear of the engine actuated the clutch. A belt driven vacuum pump supplied the vacuum to the system. The helm used a standard cable system. The heat exchanger was mounted on the starboard side near the engine. The exhaust pipe that went through the transom was to the right of the hull centreline. The air reservoir was on the port side near the bulkhead. (Ref 1)

Invader engine manufactured by the Hudson Motor Car Company under licence from Hall-Scott. This engine was used in the Eureka and early LCVPs. Despite many locations where the Hudson label appeared, it was still referred to as the Hall-Scott. (Ref 25)

RIGHT
An advertisement from 1937 for the Hall-Scott Invader engine. The Hall-Scott engines tended to overheat quickly when the strainer was clogged with sand. The Gray Marine engine did not heat up as quickly probably because of the larger iron mass of the Gray engine when compared to the Hall-Scott. (Ref 28)

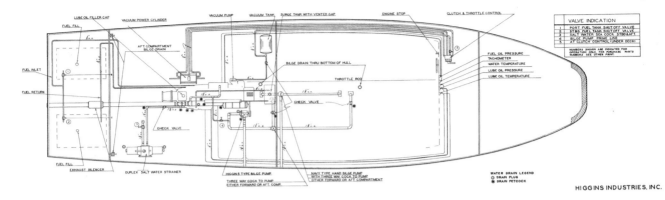

HIGGINS INDUSTRIES, INC.

The Superior Gas Engine Company

The Eureka boat with the Superior Diesel installation. As with the installation of the Hall-Scott engine, since the helm was at the front of the boat, a vacuum control system was used to operate the throttle and engine clutch. A large vacuum cylinder located to the left rear of the engine actuated the clutch. A belt driven vacuum pump supplied the vacuum to the system. The helm used a standard cable system. The heat exchanger was mounted on the starboard side near the engine. The exhaust pipe that went through the transom was to the right of the hull centreline. The air reservoir was on the port side near the bulkhead. (Ref 1)

The Superior Gas Engine Co of Springfield, Ohio had been a manufacturer of high quality internal combustion engines since 1926, with a reputation that meant it did not have to advertise extensively. During the Second World War, the company had 1800 employees and received the Maritime Commission 'M' award for quality production and the Victory Fleet Flag Award for their high production rate of marine engines. The company manufactured engines for Liberty Ships, LSTs, for lend-lease to foreign countries, for Eurekas, and to a limited extent for LCVPs. The engine used in the LCVP was a four-cylinder,

1. Supercharger	9. Reverse Gear
2. Flywheel Housing Cover	10. Reduction Gear
3. Oil Pan	11. Governor
4. Fuel Filter	12. Fuel Injection Pressure Pipe
5. Hand Hole Cover	13. Fuel Injection Nozzle
6. Fuel Pump	14. Electric Air Heater
7. Fuel Transfer Pump	15. Air Intake Pipe
8. Governor Drive Housing	16. Air Intake Cooler

1. Heat Exchanger	6. Water By-Pass Line
2. Exhaust Manifold	7. Electric Starting Motor
3. Oil Cooler	8. Air Cleaner & Silencer
4. Raw (Salt) Water Pump	9. Supercharger Inlet Pipe
5. Lub. Oil Screen Housing	10. Flywheel Housing

Superior Diesel model SMRA-4, port side view showing the location of significant components. The engine had a displacement of 366 cubic inches and developed 150hp at 2400rpm. The engine weighed 1800lbs with all fluids installed. The fuel injector pump supplied fuel pressure at 1600psi via fuel tubes to the injectors. The minimum oil viscosity used on the engine was SAE 20 but higher viscosities were recommended depending on environmental conditions. (Ref 23)

Superior Diesel engine viewed from the starboard side showing the air intake filter/silencer that is connected to the supercharger or blower. The supercharger is gear driven and assists in forcing air under pressure to the intake manifold. More modern engines use a turbocharger which is driven by a turbine in the exhaust system. Most marine diesels in Second World War landing craft used a supercharger. (Ref 23)

four-cycle, diesel engine, model SMRA-4. A unique aspect of the combustion chamber, called the dual combustion system, consisted of two combustion chambers. Both combustion chambers were open for normal operation. During starting, a valve closed access to the auxiliary combustion chamber, causing the compression ratio to increase, making cold starting easier. Cold starting of diesel engines of the era was often difficult. Since diesels rely on compression temperatures to ignite the fuel/air mixture, low temperature reduces the chance of igniting the fuel when injected. Other diesels used air heaters during starting. Also, adding a small amount of gasoline to the fuel helped cold starting by volatilizing the mixture. See Appendix C for detailed drawings of the Superior Diesel installation.

Kermath Engine Company

A few LCVPs were equipped with the Kermath gasoline engine. The Kermath Engine Company produced the 225hp Sea Wolf engine for Coast Guard picket boats during the Second World War. The V-12 Sea Raider engine was also produced for a variety of applications in the US Navy.

Kermath Sea Wolf six-cylinder marine engine used in the Eureka boat. (Ref 24)

Kermath gasoline engines were used in the Eureka, as shown in this advertisement. The Kermath Company was a large supplier of engines, both diesel and gasoline fuelled, from 25 to 500 horsepower. (4-012B, Ref 10)

An advertisement from 1942 for Kermath engines with one of the featured engines being the 225hp Sea Wolf. (Ref 29)

Gray Marine Diesel engine
Model 64-HN9, a GM Diesel
6-71 adapted for marine use.
(Ref 3)

The Gray Marine Motor Company

The most widely used power plant for the LCVP was the Gray Marine Diesel
Model 64-HN9 as specified by the Bureau of Ships, United States Navy. This
was essentially the General Motors 6-71 Diesel (later named Detroit Diesel)
engine modified for marine use. The designation 6-71 means six-cylinder
inline engine, 71 cubic inches per cylinder (actually 70.93 cubic inches). Other
engines in the 71 series included one-, two-, three-, and four-cylinder inline
designs. The engine is of two-stroke design with two exhaust valves per cylinder. The connecting rods and pistons were common to all models, reducing
the overall cost of parts inventories (bore 4.35 inches, stroke 5.0 inches). The
6-71 was first introduced by the Diesel Engine Division of General Motors
Corporation in 1938. This engine used uniflow scavenging where the fuel/air
mixture is forced into the cylinder, combustion occurs and exhaust products
exit through pushrod actuated exhaust valves at the top of the combustion
chamber. A Roots blower provided air under pressure to the cylinders. Single
injectors, one per cylinder, provided fuel under pressure at the appropriate
time to initiate combustion. Relatively low fuel pressure on the order of 10psi
was provided to the injectors, which boosted the fuel pressure to approximately
600psi at injection. The maximum engine speed was governed at 2100rpm
with a cruising speed of 1000–1400rpm.

The General Motors Detroit Diesel Division offered the 6-71 for sale in
1938. There had been considerable research and development effort at General
Motors Corporation aimed at producing a generic diesel engine that could be
used by a variety of industries such as automotive, industrial and marine. The
main incentive for GM to develop the engine was for its own truck production
and Yellow Coach power plants, but GM engineers were also looking ahead to
other applications, so the engine was designed use several different manifolds,
several different cylinder arrangements, mounting brackets and transmissions
for a variety of applications.

The 1938 vintage 71 engines were equipped with Roots blowers. Later production units were equipped with a turbocharger in series with the blower to boost horsepower. The 4-71 (four-cylinder) and 6-71 engines were produced in large quantities for landing craft, small tug boats, workboats and military vehicles such as tanks. Gray Marine entered into a contract with General Motors to adapt the 6-71 to marine use. The engine was nicknamed the 'Jimmy'. Marine engines were introduced in the three-, four- and six-cylinder design with power ratings of 85, 110 and 165hp, respectively. The engine design incorporated the fuel injector on top of each cylinder, making it a modular unit which could easily be assembled in a variety of cylinder configurations. All engines were rated at 2000rpm and shared the same bore and stroke dimensions, which reduced the complexity of parts inventory by utilizing the same parts for a variety of engines. Gray Marine received the base engine and added a cooling system with heat exchanger, oil cooler, intake air silencer, engine speed governor, instrument panel, and flywheel pulley for accessories such as a bilge pump. A transmission with 1.5:1 and 3:1 reduction gear could be supplied with the unit. Production was ramped up during the Second World War with a new facility.

See Appendix D for detailed drawings of the Gray Marine diesel installation.

Gray Marine Motor Company advertisement showing an LCVP and two LCPRs that have Gray power plants installed. (Ref 31)

Servicemen being trained on the GM Diesel 6-71 at the Gray Marine Plant in Detroit. These are machinist mates often called 'motor macs' whose responsibility in the LCVP was the proper operation of the engine. (Ref 30)

Advertisement for the GM Diesel 6-71. Later GM Diesel became Detroit Diesel. (Ref 25)

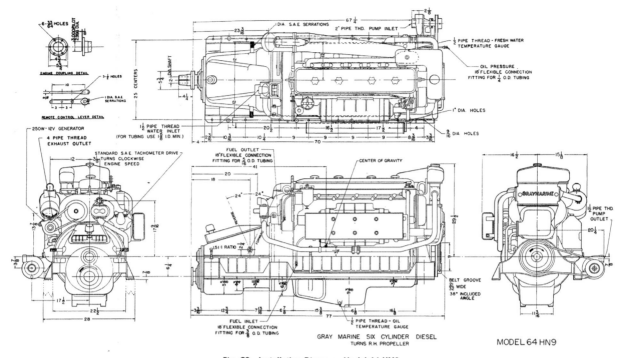

Fig. C2—Installation Diagram, Model 64-HN9.
Typical Landing Boat Engine, with deep sump oil pan and short propeller coupling. The bilge pump and exhaust elbow are not found on all models.

Drawing of the Gray Marine model 64-HN9 with transmission turning
the propeller clockwise when looking toward the bow. (Ref 3)

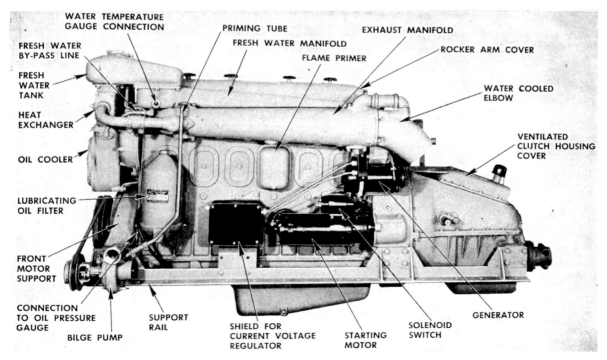

The port side view of the 64-HN9 with major components labelled. (Ref 3)

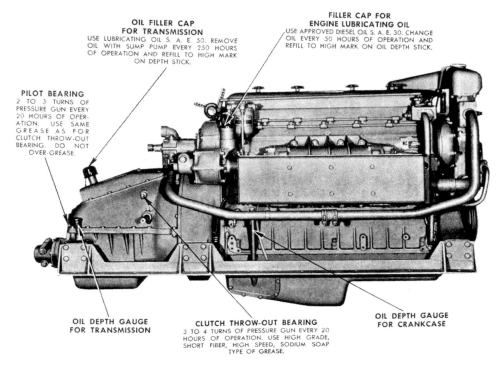

OIL FILLER CAP FOR TRANSMISSION
USE LUBRICATING OIL S. A. E. 50. REMOVE OIL WITH SUMP PUMP EVERY 250 HOURS OF OPERATION AND REFILL TO HIGH MARK ON DEPTH STICK.

FILLER CAP FOR ENGINE LUBRICATING OIL
USE APPROVED DIESEL OIL S. A. E. 30. CHANGE OIL EVERY 50 HOURS OF OPERATION AND REFILL TO HIGH MARK ON OIL DEPTH STICK.

PILOT BEARING
2 TO 3 TURNS OF PRESSURE GUN EVERY 20 HOURS OF OPERATION. USE SAME GREASE AS FOR CLUTCH THROW-OUT BEARING. DO NOT OVER-GREASE.

OIL DEPTH GAUGE FOR TRANSMISSION

CLUTCH THROW-OUT BEARING
3 TO 4 TURNS OF PRESSURE GUN EVERY 20 HOURS OF OPERATION. USE HIGH GRADE, SHORT FIBER, HIGH SPEED, SODIUM SOAP TYPE OF GREASE.

OIL DEPTH GAUGE FOR CRANKCASE

Starboard view of the 64-HN9 with major components labelled. (Ref 3)

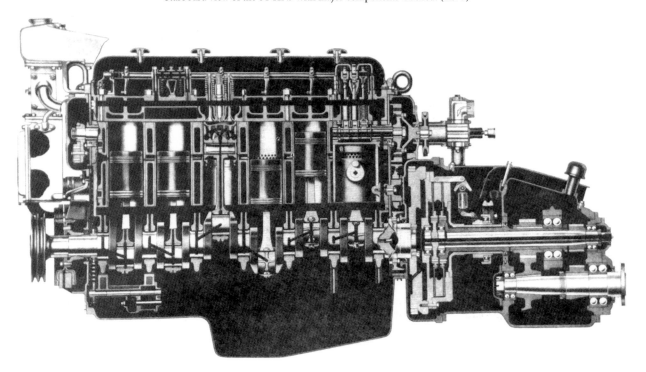

Cross-sectional view of the 64-HN9 engine and transmission. (Ref 3)

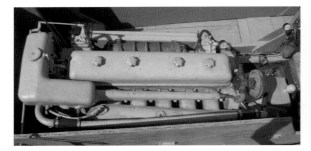

ABOVE

Right side of the engine showing the Roots blower assembly and silencer. To the upper right is the engine governor and throttle linkage. (Ref 10)

TOP

Top view of the engine in the enclosure or 'dog house' showing the valve cover and secondary cooling system reservoir. The multiple knobs on the valve cover were for ease of removal for quick adjustment of the valve rocker arms and other maintenance. (Ref 10)

ABOVE

View of Roots blower with silencer removed. Air enters these ports and is forced into the combustion chambers. (Ref 10)

RIGHT

A cross-sectional view of the engine showing the blower and air circulation path through the engine along with related parts. This is a crankcase scavenged engine where exhaust products are expelled through the exhaust valves while simultaneously drawing in fresh air through the crankcase. (Ref 3)

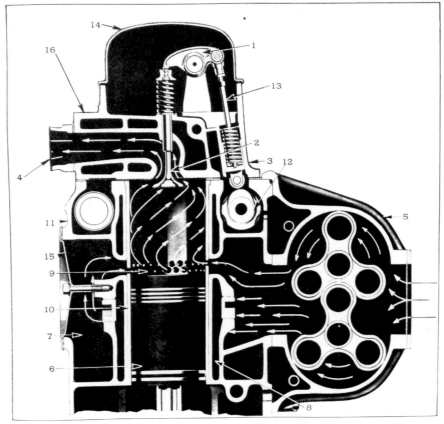

Fig. O1—Air Intake System Through Blower and Engine.

1. Exhaust Valve Rocker	5. Blower	9. Port—Admitting Air to Cylinder	13. Push Rod
2. Exhaust Valve	6. Piston	10. Cylinder Liner	14. Rocker Cover
3. Cylinder Head	7. Air Box	11. Cylinder Block	15. Hand Hole Cover
4. Exhaust Manifold	8. Cooling-Water Passage	12. Camshaft	16. Water Manifold

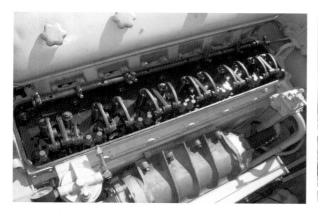

Cylinder head with fuel lines, rocker shaft and fuel injectors removed. (Ref 10)

Close-up of the rocker arms with the rocker shafts removed. There are two exhaust valve rocker arms and one fuel injector rocker arm per cylinder. (Ref 10)

Propeller shaft coupling and feeler gauge used to check the consistency of the gap around the coupling which indicates proper alignment. The parts shown are the propeller shaft coupling (1), the transmission drive flange (2), and the feeler gauge (3) used to check the gap between the two pieces. The feeler gauge size is 0.002 inches. The gap between the drive flange and coupling should not exceed 0.002 inches, which indicates good engine alignment with the propeller shaft. Poor alignment can cause excessive vibration, loosening of the fittings and damage to the stuffing box (shaft seal). This alignment check had to be performed periodically since the wood hull would change dimensions slightly as a result of loading from cargo, wave action and moisture related swelling of the wood. (Ref 3)

Fig. C6—Checking Engine Alignment at Propeller Coupling.

1. Propeller Coupling   2. Countershaft   3. Feeler Gauge

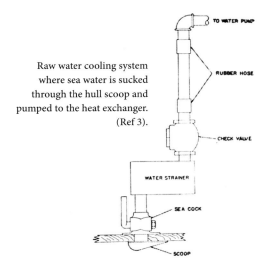

Raw water cooling system where sea water is sucked through the hull scoop and pumped to the heat exchanger. (Ref 3).

Water strainer manufactured with 'Higgins' cast into the fitting. The plastic transparent cover houses the strainer. The screw at the top allows dismantling and cleaning. Every time an LCVP landed on shore, a crewman had to remove the screen and clean out the sand to prevent overheating from restricted water flow. The strainer shown to the right has a port on the bottom that can house another strainer. By turning the valve handle 180 degrees the spare strainer can be selected while the other is cleaned. (Ref 10)

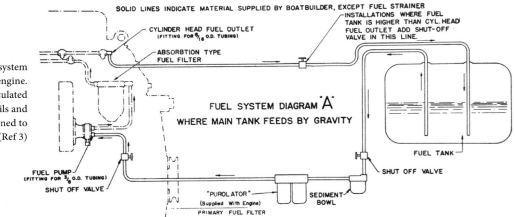

Fuel delivery system for the diesel engine. The fuel was circulated through rails and unused fuel returned to the fuel tank. (Ref 3)

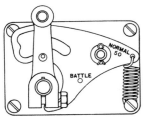

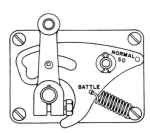

ATTACH SPRING TO BATTLE RATING POSITION FOR MAX. FUEL INJECTION.

ATTACH SPRING TO NORMAL RATING POSITION FOR LIMITED FUEL INJECTION.

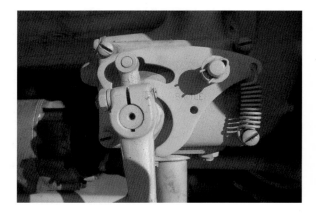

Governor setting for the engine. The normal setting to the right limits the engine revolutions to around 2000rpm. The battle setting on the left allows a higher rpm which will cause additional wear on the engine if used for an extensive period of time. Ref 3)

Photo of a governor set at normal. In the normal position, the roller cannot ride over the hump to increase the rpm. With the spring in the battle position, the roller easily rides over the hump to obtain higher rpm. (Ref 10)

Coolant and raw water circulation system through the engine. Sea water is pumped to a heat exchanger which cools the engine via an internal coolant separate from sea water. (Ref 3)

Fig. N1—Water Circulating System.

1. Fresh Water Tank	4. Heat Exchanger Drain Plug	7. Oil Cooler Outlet Line
2. Heat Exchanger	5. Oil Cooler	8. Fresh Water Pump
3. Zinc Electrodes	6. Oil Cooler Intake Line	9. Sea Water Line
		10. Sea Water Pump

BELOW

Right side of engine showing silencer, breather and governor housing where the operator selects either normal or battle operation. The breather feeds crankcase gases into the air-intake through the silencer housing. (Ref 3)

Fig. M14—Forward End of Engine.

1. Fresh Water Tank	3. Oil Cooler
2. Heat Exchanger	4. Fresh Water By-Pass Line

Heat exchanger used for cooling the engine. Engine coolant is circulated through the heat exchanger while raw sea water flows though the cooling side of the heat exchanger, thereby isolating the engine from corrosive sea water. (Ref 3)

Engine oil delivery diagram for the 6-71. (Ref 3)

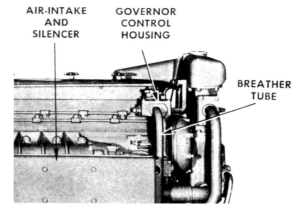

AIR-INTAKE AND SILENCER

GOVERNOR CONTROL HOUSING

BREATHER TUBE

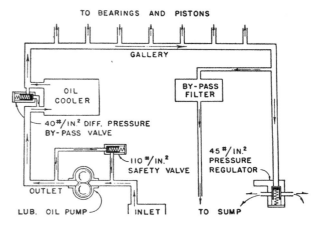

TO BEARINGS AND PISTONS

GALLERY

OIL COOLER

BY-PASS FILTER

40#/IN.^{2} DIFF. PRESSURE BY-PASS VALVE

110#/IN.^{2} SAFETY VALVE

45#/IN.^{2} PRESSURE REGULATOR

OUTLET

LUB. OIL PUMP

INLET

TO SUMP

The Delco starter used on the GM Diesel engine. A solenoid actuates the Bendix drive to engage the starter pinion in the engine gear. In case of solenoid failure, a pry bar can be used to push the shift lever to operate the starter. (Ref 3)

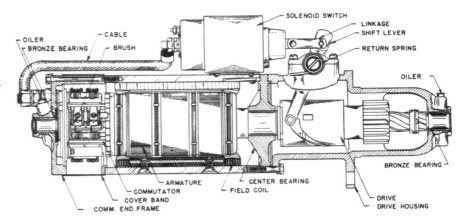

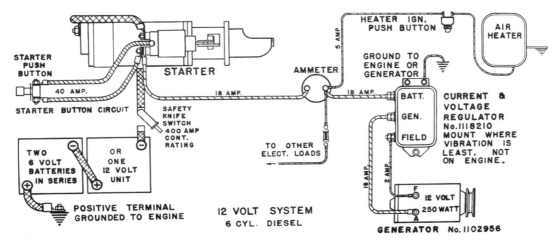

LCVP electrical circuit, which functions as a generator that supplies power to charge the starter motor battery and also to operate a combustion air heater for the engine to aid in cold starts. (Ref 3)

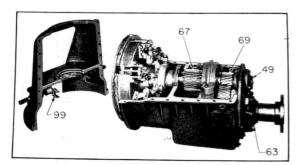

Fig. T8—Upper Half of Housing Removed.

49. Retainer—Reverse Shaft Bearing.
63. Retainer—Countershaft Bearing
67. Pinion—Forward
69. Pinion—Reverse
99. Operating Yoke—Throw-Out Fork

Major components of the twin-disc type transmission. (Ref 3)

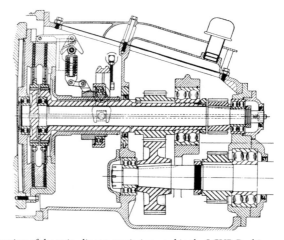

Drawing of the twin-disc transmission used in the LCVP. Pushing the pressure plate forward to engage the front disc causes the propeller to rotate to give a forward velocity to the craft. Pulling back on the pressure plate engages the rear disc that causes the propeller shaft to rotate in the opposite or reverse direction. (Ref 3)

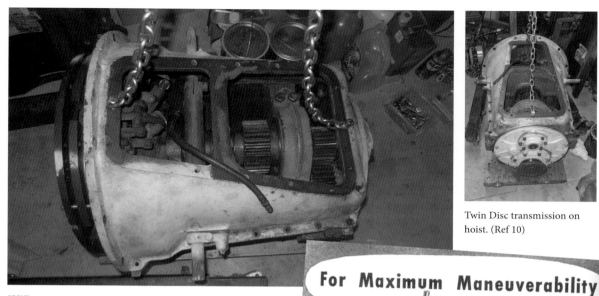

Twin Disc transmission on hoist. (Ref 10)

ABOVE

View of the twin disc type transmission which consists of a forward gear, neutral position and reverse gear. Transmissions were manufactured by the Twin Disc Clutch Company, Racine, Wisconsin and Borg-Warner Corporation, Detroit, Michigan. Gear reduction ratio was 1.5:1. The transmissions contained helical gears, spur gears or a combination of the two depending on manufacturer. Some transmissions were water cooled and some were air cooled. There were transmissions for both left hand and right hand rotation of the propeller. (Ref 10)

RIGHT

Twin Disc advertisement for the transmission. (Ref 32)

View of the actuator for the twin disc clutch assembly within the transmission. (Ref 10)

View of countershaft, bearing and gears within the Twin Disc transmission. (Ref 10)

Borg-Warner Series 60
Transmission with single
clutch disc used in the LCVP.
(Ref 40)

1. Input shaft
2. Access port
3. Release bearing cap
4. Release bearing cap lock
5. Release bearing cap bolt
6. Clutch release arm
7. Shift lever shaft clamp bolt
8. Shift lever clamp nut
9. Shift lever clamp

10. Drain plug
11. Shift lever shaft
12. Clutch release arm shaft
13. Gear shaft retaining bolt
15. Gear shaft retaining lock
    washer
16. Propeller shaft drive flange
17. Shift stop bracket
18. Bolt

19. Gear shaft
20. Clutch bearing sleeve
    housing
21. Clutch yoke spring
22. Clutch bearing sleeve cap
23. Clutch release bearing sleeve
24. Clutch sleeve cap lock
25. Clutch sleeve cap screw
26. Vent

The other transmission manufacturer was the Detroit Gear and Aircraft Parts Division of Borg-Warner Corporation in Detroit. This was a water-cooled transmission with a reduction ratio of 1.50:1. This transmission was supplied with the 64-HN5 diesel. A heat exchanger was provided at the bottom of the oil sump for cooling.

Performance and Handling

The LCVP was designed to travel through surf, run up on a beach, lower a ramp and rapidly unload troops. The LCVP handled quite well, turning easily within its own length when going ahead. However, when retracting from a beach or backing up, skill was required to maintain course, since the craft would spin readily because it had no forward keel. The LCVP attained its maximum speed of approximately 12 knots when empty with the bow ramp up and out of the water. When fully loaded, the lower portion of the bow would become submerged resulting in ploughing through the water and a maximum speed of approximately 9 knots. As typical of a craft 36 feet in length, it would pitch and roll in a seaway, causing many of the troops to become seasick. When the bow was ploughing through seas, water would spray into the occupant compartment causing the single bilge pump to be working continuously (the bilge pump intake is in the bilge at the lowest part of the hull amidships). The craft was vulnerable to swamping if the ramp was not completely retracted and secured. Under certain sea conditions, a partially retracted ramp could allow water to flood the forward bilge causing the hull to float bow down. This was a dangerous, unstable condition, since the bow-down mode allowed more water to enter and flood the craft, eventually causing it to sink by the head. This happened often so the Navy decided to fill the bilges of LCVPs with foam after the war to reduce the chance of swamping the craft.

CHAPTER 5

A newly completed boat being lowered into the bayou. Notice the soft chine (rounded edges) at the stern which indicates this to be an early Higgins boat. These were later changed to hard chines since other manufacturers could not replicate the curved shape. (Ref 2)

Early instruction manuals on the operation of the LCVP depicted the craft above. The upper photo shows the boat cover tarpaulin with its support beams on the cargo deck. The machine gun fittings have not been installed. The lower photo shows a large vision slot at the bow ramp. The calm waters suggest these photos were taken on a lake or bayou near the Higgins plant in New Orleans. (Ref 4)

Fig. 5-- Crew of an LCVP-- (1) Coxswain, (2) engineman, (3) seaman.

Fig. 6-- How an LCVP transports 3/4 ton weapons carrier. The two scarfings just aft the engine hatch are manned by the LCVP's own crew when other personnel is not available.

The instruction manual illustrations show the crew positions and a ¾-ton WC (Weapons Carrier), the largest vehicle that could be transported. The coxswain was the captain of the craft, while the machinist mate handled the engine and two seamen handled mooring lines. The seamen also operated the machine guns. (Ref 4)

The LCVP was designed to be stowed on a large ship and launched from a davit or by a crane. When launching, the craft was empty except for the crew. With a davit, the cables were attached to the bow shackle and the stern shackle located amidships. When launching from a crane, a three-point cable lift was used, with a point connected to the bow shackle and each of two stern shackles in the crew compartment. Manuals were developed to train personnel in the handling and maintenance of the boat.

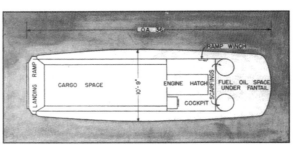

Fig. 3-- General layout and principal dimensions of LCVP.

ABOVE

LCVP with maximum load of 36 troops. A rifle platoon in the Second World War typically consisted of 48 troops, which meant that units were divided into different boats as a result of the 36-troop limitation. (Ref 4)

RIGHT

Navy instruction manuals presented the basic configuration of the LCVP. Dimensions and crew positions are shown in the illustrations. (Ref 4)

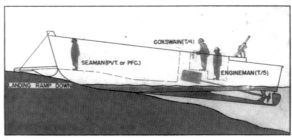

Fig. 4— LCVP profile sketch showing lines of hull. The boat is beached and the ramp lowered.

Gear shift/throttle handle. The handle was twisted counter clockwise to increase engine speed and clockwise to decrease engine speed. A small knob at the base limited twist so the engine would not shut off. Lifting the knob and twisting clockwise would shut off the engine. The handle was pushed forward for forward gear or pulled back for reverse. (Ref 10)

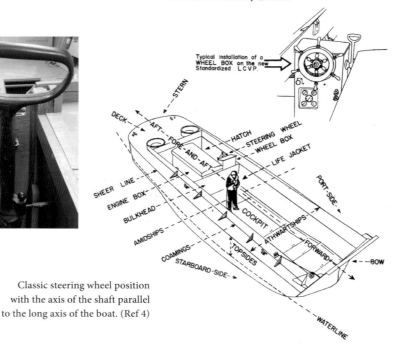

Classic steering wheel position with the axis of the shaft parallel to the long axis of the boat. (Ref 4)

FAR LEFT
Classic marine steering wheel. (Ref 10)

LEFT
The wheel box with the truck style steering wheel, which was the most common on the LCVPs. The steering wheel shaft telescopes upward to adjust for the height of the coxswain. (Ref 10).

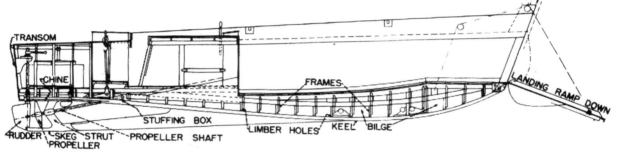

Diagram used for training Navy personnel on the various components of an LCVP. These are drawings of an early LCVP as indicated by the classic steering wheel at the wheel box. (Ref 4)

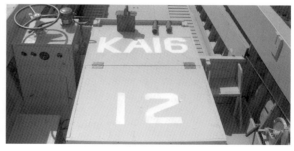

ABOVE
Typical crew compartment for an LCVP. The winch is internal and to the right. Engine controls and steering box are to the left. The 'dog house' or engine box in the middle houses the engine. (Ref 10)

LEFT
View of the cargo compartment from the bow showing life preserver rack on the right and the equalizer pulley box on the left. (Ref 10)

TOP LEFT

View of crew compartment from the bow showing the bulkhead and fire extinguisher. (Ref 10)

TOP RIGHT

Cargo compartment showing tread planks used to increase traction on the vehicle track. (Ref 10)

ABOVE

A 1943 vintage LCVP cruising at 3 knots unloaded. The identification code indicates that the craft is No 12 from AKA-16, the attack cargo ship USS *Aquarius*. This ship saw extensive service in many Pacific amphibious operations, earning eight battle stars. (Ref 10)

RIGHT TOP

WC-51 Weapons Carrier ¾-ton truck loaded on an LCVP. (Ref 26)

RIGHT

A 1943 vintage LCVP landing in calm water at a concrete launching ramp. (Ref 10)

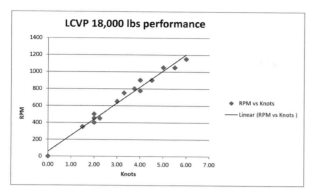

LCVP 18,000 lbs performance

Engine revolutions versus boat speed for an 18,000lb LCVP with a 22in propeller. The transmission gear reduction is 1.51:1 to the propeller. The maximum published speed of the LCVP is approximately 12 knots, although veterans' accounts suggest that this was rarely achieved. Based on this curve and extrapolating to 2100rpm, the governed speed of the engine, the maximum speed is 10.5 knots. (Ref 10)

ABOVE
Red weather warning flags used during the Second World War. (Ref 4)

Handling in windy conditions was discussed extensively with boat crews. When the craft was empty and hove-to (stopped), the wind would quickly push the boat down wind, although when fully loaded, the effect was less. The influence of current is a significant aspect of handling any craft, and the cox was trained to study the currents in the area of operation and adjust the craft angle and speed accordingly. When attempting to beach or come alongside a wharf, the current might push the boat at an excessive speed. Reducing the engine speed reduces boat speed but also reduces manoeuvring capability, which depends on speed of water flow past the rudder. Approaching against the current helps with control but the cox needed to use good judgement while landing. The downwind landing poses the same set of problems in that in order to cut speed, engine speed is reduced and steerage becomes less effective.

Boat crews were taught that the LCVP had to be handled gently since the rudder was small and a significant flow of water over the rudder was required in order to get the vessel to respond. Also, when backing, there was a significant propeller wash that could disturb other craft nearby while in harbour. While going astern, the LCVP would tend to spin (swing) easily, so caution needed to be exercised in not backing up too quickly. The manoeuvring rudder was small but helped in reversing the craft.

BOTTOM
These sketches from the manual taught the coxswain how to handle the boat without losing control caused by quickly spinning the boat. The LCVP would pivot easily since it had no keel toward the bow. Backing slowly with the appropriate rudder position, avoided loss of control from rapid spinning. (Ref 4)

BELOW
Backing too fast caused a quick pivoting (spinning) of the boat and loss of control. (Ref 4)

Fig. 180-- Watch your wash; never do this.

A drawing cautioning the coxswain to travel slowly to keep the wake from disturbing other craft while in harbour. (Ref 4)

Fig. 184-- Turn like this, swinging slowly, maintaining control.

(A) Normal use of anti-broaching lines when a landing boat is perpendicular to the beach.

(C) Use of anti-broaching lines when the bow is floating free due to irregularities in the beach.

(B) Use of anti-broaching lines when a landing boat has broached to port. Note that the port line is slack but kept well clear of the screw. When a boat broaches to starboard the use of lines is reversed.

ABOVE

Diagram showing how to reduce the chance of broaching by using ropes to steady the craft. (Ref 5)

BELOW

Diagram showing how broaching on shore can occur. To avoid this the LCVP should always land perpendicular to the waves even though the hull may not be perpendicular to the shore. (Ref 10)

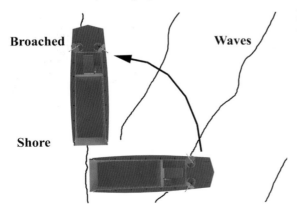

Broaching is a problem with small craft such as the LCVP. Broaching is the condition where the craft rotates 90 degrees to the original orientation of the craft. This is typically a result of wave action. Broaching at the shore is shown in the diagram to the lower left. With the bow engaged on the beach and the stern free of the bottom, wave action can push the stern toward the shore, resulting in a change in orientation of the LCVP. If this continues, the craft will be parallel to the shore, making it virtually impossible to move. When broached on shore, the propeller is usually out or partially out of the water, providing a lack of thrust to withdraw the craft. Wave action also pushes the hull on shore, driving the bottom into the sand, making it very difficult to move. The hull can only swing one way to disengage from shore.

Broaching at sea is also a problem. Shown to the right is a drawing of the LCVP with a following sea. As the craft starts to surf down a wave, the bow can dig in and the hull will tend to yaw toward the starboard or port side. This results in a loss of steerageway, and the hull could end up in the wave trough broadside-on to the direction of the wave velocity. In the trough, the craft will roll severely to the point of possibly swamping or capsizing. Consequently, the coxswain must steer carefully to ensure that the hull travels straight down the wave. With steep waves (high amplitude) there is a tendency to bury the bow in the trough, which can also swamp the boat. When going upwind, the craft should proceed directly into the waves to minimize the tendency to roll.

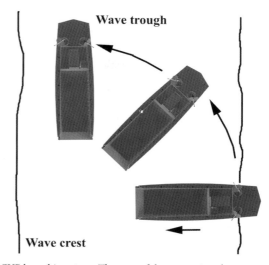

Wave trough

Wave crest

LCVP broaching at sea. The crest of the wave raises the stern causing the hull to surf and increase speed. The bow tends to dig into the next wave and causes difficulty in steering which requires considerable helmsmanship on the part of the coxswain to maintain control. (Ref 10)

Go slow and let her lift over the big ones.

Fig. 196-- Never run into the troughs. You'll get wet and you'll roll terribly.

Don't drive into heavy seas. Go easy.

When in heavy seas with high wave height relative to wave length there was a tendency to bury the bow in a wave, causing swamping when heading into the sea. The coxswain was cautioned to reduce speed so that the hull rides up over the wave and not through it. Swamping by the bow in this craft results in a nose-down attitude that might increase water entry into the hull, to the point where the bilge pumps would have insufficient capacity to prevent sinking. After the war the Navy filled the bilges of these boats with foam to prevent sinking by the bow. (Ref 4)

Fig. 195-- Head directly into heavy seas.

Boat handling in heavy seas as taught to the coxswain in the training manual. The lesson here is to avoid running into a trough if possible to reduce rolling and water spray into the hull. (Ref 4)

This page appears in an instruction manual on the operation of the LCVP. The top drawing cautions the cox not to ride a wave into shore lest the boat broach as a result of the surf pushing on the stern. The next drawing warns not to drop the ramp too early and to make sure the boat is properly grounded prior to release of the ramp. The next drawing cautions not to allow the hull to broadside the surf lest the boat capsize. Finally, the last drawing of a sunken craft demonstrates the result of forgetting to immediately secure the ramp before retracting. (Ref 5)

BELOW

This drawing cautions the coxswain not to drop the ramp too early, while the boat still has headway, which can damage the ramp hinge making it virtually impossible to drive the boat back out to sea. A damaged ramp not sealing properly will take on water rapidly and swamp the boat. (Ref 4)

When boarding an LCVP from scrambling nets, the disembarking troops from the transport ship were told to loosen straps on their packs and have their rifles slung in a manner such that if a soldier fell into the water, the heavy equipment could be quickly released. Troops were taught to go over the side left leg first and to use the vertical line in the net as hand holds. Wave action made loading of troops very dangerous as they had to gauge when to jump into the boat at the highest point of the wave.

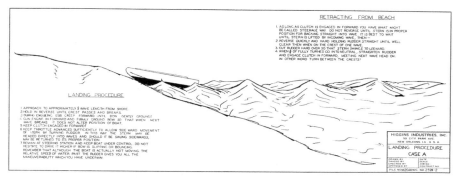

When landing on a beach with a steep slope into deep water, the LCVP must be driven hard onto the shore to secure the hull in the sand to prevent waves from broaching the boat, as described earlier. (Ref 4)

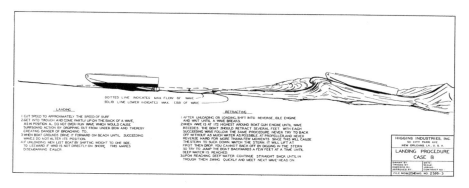

This sketch teaches the coxswain to approach a shallow beach without a sand bar at the speed of the waves and allow successive waves to help ground the boat. (Ref 4)

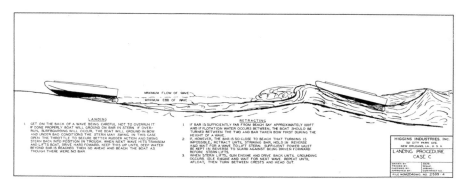

In this example the beach has a bar, and the coxswain is taught to run onto the sandbar, wait for the next wave to lift the boat over the bar, and then beach the boat in a normal fashion. (Ref 4)

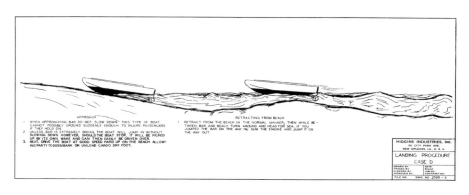

This sketch teaches the coxswain how to run the craft over the sandbar if there is little surf. If the boat slows or stops, the stern wake will lift the hull over the sandbar when there is no wave action to help. (Ref 4)

CHAPTER 6

Wartime Service

BELOW
LCVP No 18 from the attack transport USS *Newberry* (APA-158), possibly at Iwo Jima with a maximum load of troops. Ref 26)

BOTTOM LEFT
LCV unloading a ¾-ton truck. (Ref 15)

BELOW RIGHT
LCVPs departing for shore during the landings on Bougainville, Solomon Islands, in November 1943. (Ref 26)

During the Second World War the LCVP was used in almost all theatres, including North Africa, Sicily, mainland Europe, the Pacific and the Far East. As a result, there are many veterans' accounts of their experience of landing from an LCVP. Seasickness was rampant and oftentimes troops stepped off the ramp in deep water – sometimes over their heads – because obstructions and other debris prevented the LCVP from reaching the beach itself. Boarding an LCVP was difficult in heavy seas using the scrambling nets as ladders. One had to judge when to let go and jump into the boat at the highest point in the wave. The side armour was limited in extent so when during an opposed landing, troops had to hunker down to benefit from the armour protection. But once beached, the LCVP could be quickly unloaded, much faster than many of its competitors. When leaving the craft, troops in columns were told to jump out to one side or the other of the ramp since there was a possibility that the boat would move forward as it became lighter and the wave action pushed it in further, risking injury to any soldier directly in front of the ramp.

LCVP being lowered into the water with a three-point cable during the invasion of Sicily, 1943. (Ref 26).

LEFT AND BELOW

A three-point cable is being used to lower an LCVP onto a cradle. (Ref 10)
The photo below shows an LCVP being lowered using davits on the side of a ship. (Ref 38)

TOP

LST-541 (Landing Ship Tank) at anchor off Le Havre, France in May 1945. This illustrates a typical layout of davits on an LST. (Ref 41)

ABOVE

Looking toward the bow of *LST-541* sailing up the Seine River in France, March 1945. The LCVPs are stowed with the davit trolleys in the raised position. When launching LCVPs, the trolleys slide down their rails to clear the LST hull and then the LCVPs are lowered via block and tackle. (Ref 41)

RIGHT

Close-up of the stern of an LCVP showing the rear davit arm and hoist block and tackle hooked to the stern lifting shackle. Note the rain cover over the gyro flux gate compass transmitter unit just abaft the towing post. The photo was taken from *LST-541* as it entered Le Havre, France in March 1945. The breakwater shows a German gun emplacement. (Ref 41)

The attack transport USS *Thomas Stone* (APA-29, originally AP-59) showing LCVPs stowed on davits either side of the amidships superstructure. The APA (Auxiliary Personnel Attack) was the primary assault ship that carried troops and landing craft to the debarkation area before the troops were transferred to the landing craft for an amphibious attack. The LCVPs were launched with crew on board and then loaded with troops via netting on the side of the hull. The derricks were used to lower equipment into the LCVPs such as jeeps, ammunition or light artillery. (Ref 43)

BELOW

USS *Aquarius* (AKA-16: Auxiliary Cargo Attack) in the south Pacific. Unlike APAs, attack cargo ships were not originally intended to carry troops direct to the assault beaches, but were designed to transport cargo and vehicles; in practice, the roles overlapped. AKAs carried LCVPs on davits and stacked on deck, with heavy-lift derricks used to lower LCVPs and cargo. When docking facilities were available, the derricks were used to unload cargo directly onto the quay. (Ref 26)

RIGHT
LCVP No 22 from AKA-16, *Aquarius*, somewhere in the south Pacific. (Ref 26)

APD-1 (Auxiliary Personnel Destroyer) USS *Manley* was a high-speed transport. APDs 1–36 were converted First World War flush-deck destroyers of the *Wickes*, *Clemson* and *Caldwell* classes. The torpedo tubes and forward boilers (with the two funnels that served them) were removed to make room for davits which held LCVPs. The purpose of the APD was to deliver a specialized company sized unit such as Marine Raiders, Underwater Demolition Teams (UDT) and Army Rangers to enemy-held shores. Despite the reduction in boiler power, the ADP was still capable of the relatively high speed of 26 knots, which was required by its raiding mission into hostile areas. (Ref 17)

RIGHT

LCPR No 1 from the USS *Humphreys* (APD-12) coming alongside probably to be hoisted by the davits. This LCPR is carrying a UDT (Underwater Demolition Team) returning from a mission off Leyte in 1944 searching for mines and other underwater obstacles. (Ref 44)

BELOW

LCVP No 22 from USS *Dickman* (APA-13) at Normandy. Note the safety lines hanging from the side in case someone falls overboard. (Ref 26).

In preparation for an assault landing on a beachhead, a complete checkout of the boat, including installing drain plugs, was carried out, just before the LCVPs were off-loaded from the parent attack transport (APA; the largest of these carried over twenty LCVPs). Just before the LCVP was lowered into the sea, the engine was started to make sure it was running properly. Once on the water, the forward and aft falls (block and tackle) were released, and the LCVP then moved out to a holding pattern circle as shown below. The holding pattern to starboard circled clockwise; that to port, counter clockwise. Spacing between boats in a holding circle was approximately one and one half boat lengths, with speed kept to the minimum that allowed steerageway, which might vary depending on wind and sea conditions. As space became available alongside the APA, an LCVP was called in to load troops. The loading stations alongside the APA were marked with a colour code and number and had a net in position for the troops to use when climbing down into the boat. After loading, the LCVP then went back to the holding circle at the assembly area.

BELOW
Photo of a Eureka boat fitted out as a support boat. (Ref 26)

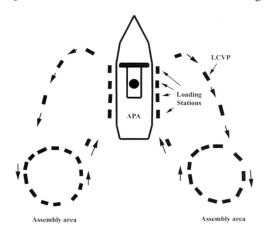

TOP LEFT
Assembly formation of LCVPs. (Ref 10)

LEFT
Landing flotilla circling at the assembly area. (Ref 26)

After all boats in the assembly area were loaded, the command was then given to move to the rendezvous area. The LCVPs peeled off, being led by a control boat that guided the flotilla to the rendezvous. The control boat was typically a Eureka boat modified with a cabin, communication and radar equipment. The single line ahead formation makes it easy to direct the LCVPs to the rendezvous area. However, if there were a threat of air attack, the LCVPs would scatter and follow in the general direction of the control boat. The flotilla was flanked by support boats, which might carry rockets for the assault, smoke screen equipment or heavy weapons to back-up the flotilla. The support craft might be modified Eureka boats or Patrol Torpedo (PT) boats. The two control boats that define the rendezvous area are shown at the top of the figure. The LCVPs line up in a flank or wave formation when reaching the rendezvous.

BELOW
Waves of landing craft approaching the beach at Iwo Jima. (Ref 26)

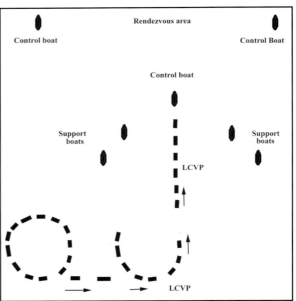

ABOVE RIGHT
Plan of formation for moving to the rendezvous area. (Ref 10)

RIGHT
LCVP assault wave waiting at the line of departure for the command to hit the beach. (Ref 10)

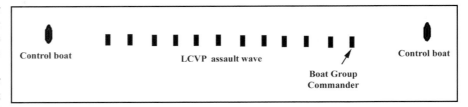

Shown above is the assault wave at the line of departure, ready to hit the beach. The boats are sitting at idle and will proceed at the signal to attack. When the signal is given, the wave starts toward the beach at about 3/4 power keeping the wave lined up. After the support boats have delivered their ordinance, the command is given for full throttle and the LCVPs proceed to the beach at maximum speed.

Scrambling nets used to allow troops to descend into LCVPs. (Ref 26)

A very famous shot of troops going ashore from a LCVP on D-Day, Normandy, June 1944. (Ref 26).

LCVP on the way to Normandy, June 1944. (Ref 26)

ABOVE
Crew handling a bow line in order to prevent the craft from broaching. (Ref 26)

RIGHT
Normandy casualties, 8 June 1944, on their way back to the troopship by LCVP. (Ref 26)

The command to deploy the LCVPs is 'Away all boats'. Large derricks were used to lower the LCVP from either an AKA or an APA transport, using a three-point lifting cable attached to a shackle forward and two shackles aft. Typically, the crew was lowered with the LCVP, and cargo was loaded later once the craft was floating and operating under its own power. Troops would climb down rope nets to board the boat. (Ref 26)

US Army LCVP with gun pits removed, Manilla Bay, 1947. After the war, the Navy declared the rear gun pits unnecessary and decked over the gun pit openings. (Ref 10)

APPENDIX A

36ft Ramp Type Eureka Landing Boat. Hall-Scott Engine Installation. Fresh Water Cooled Only with V-Drive. (Ref 1)

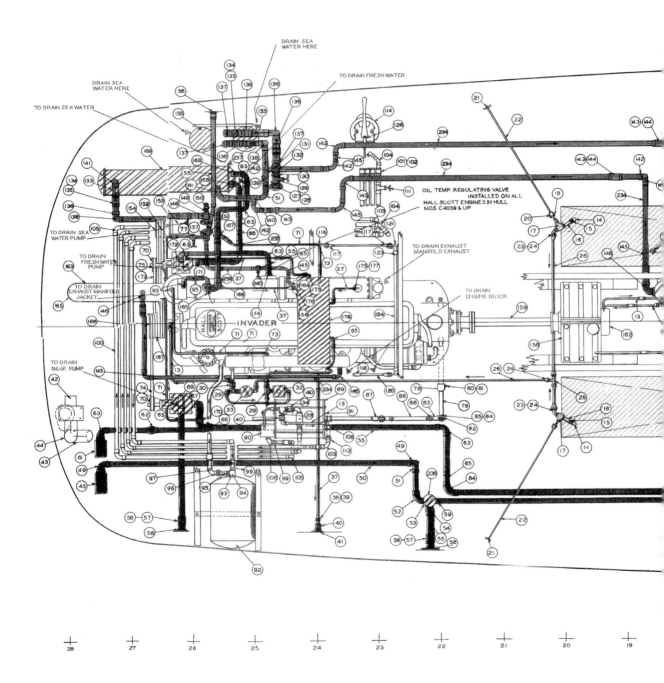

NOTE

FOR PARTS AND PRICE LIST REFER
TO SECTION VIII OF SUPPLEMENT
TO PARTS CATALOG No. 106,
TITLED HIGGINS INSTALLATION
HALL SCOTT MOTOR 36' VEHICLE
CARRIER FRESH WATER COOLED.

TO DRAIN SEA WATER FROM
VEE DRIVE OIL COOLER LINE

TO DRAIN
BILGE LINE

FRAME NUMBERS

| 17 | 16 | 15 | 14 | 13 | 12 | 11 |

SALT   WATER
FRESH WATER
GASOLINE
VACUUM
BILGE
AIR
LUBE OIL

COLD WEATHER DRAINS

HIGGINS INDUSTRIES, INC.
521 CITY PARK AVENUE
NEW ORLEANS, LA., U.S.A.

**36 FT. RAMP TYPE
EUREKA LANDING BOAT**
HALL   SCOTT   INSTALLATION
FRESH   WATER   COOLED   ONLY

DRAWN BY: A. S. TATE	DATE: 10-27-41
TRACED BY: J. MONTZ	SCALE: 1½" 1'-0"
CHECKED BY:	JOB NO:
APPROVED BY:	CONTRACT NO:
FILE NO.	DWG. NO. 2585-7E

Parts List

Figure number VC1F refers to item 1 in the diagram on the previous page.

PART #	FIGURE #	NAME	NO.REQD.	MATERIAL
H36LBHS216	VC1F	2" Protector Seal Cap	2	Brass
H36LBHS214	VC2F	2" D x 8" Pipe	2	Brass
H36LBHS215	VC3F	2-3/8" I.D. Radiator Hose	12"	Rubber
	VC4F	2" D x 30" Pipe	2	Galv.
	VC5F	2" Ell (Screwed)	2	Galv.
	VC6F	2" D x 19" Nipple	2	Galv.
H36LBHS83	VC7F	1-1/2" Plug (Screwed)	2	Brass
H36LBHS88	VC8F	3/8" T x 1/4" P Flared Half Union	4	Brass
	VC9F	3" Hose Clamps	4	Galv.
H36LBHS231	VC10F	Gas Tanks	2	St.Steel
H36LBHS81	VC11F	3/8" T x 1/4" P Flared Ell	8	Brass
H36LBHS82	VC12F	3/8" Flared Tubing Nut	14	Brass
H36LBHS90	VC13F	1/4" I.D. Copper Tubing	17'	Copper
H36LBHS73	VC14F	1/2" St. Ell (Screwed)	2	Brass
H36LBHS94	VC15F	1/2" x 3/8" Bushing (Screwed)	2	Brass
H36LBHS95	VC16F	3/8" x 2" Nipple	2	Brass
H36LBHS96	VC17F	3/8" Gas Valves	2	Brass
H36LBHS158	VC18F	3/16" x 1-3/8" D Brass Disc	2	Brass
H36LBHS155	VC19F	3/32" x 1/2" Cotter Key	2	Brass
H36LBHS156	VC20F	1/4" x 3" Brass Rod	2	Brass
H36LBHS159	VC21F	#12-24 Hex. Nuts	2	Brass
	VC22F	5/16" x 19" Brass Rod	2	Brass
H36LBHS97	VC23F	1/2" T x 3/8" P Flared Ell	3	Brass
H36LBHS98	VC24F	1/2" Flared Tubing Nut	6	Brass
	VC25F	1/2" Flared Tubing Tee	1	Brass
H36LBHS93	VC26F	1/2" O.D. Copper Tubing	15'	Copper
H36LBHS84	VC27F	3/8" x 1/4" Bushing (Screwed)		
H36LBHS106	VC28F	1/4" Close Nipple	5	Brass
H36LBHS85	VC29F	1/4" Tee (Screwed)	3	Brass
H36LBHS107	VC30F	1/4" Ball Check (Screwed)	1	Brass
H36LBHS295	VC31F	3/8" x 3/8" Flared Ell	1	Brass
H36LBHS283	VC32F	1/4" Auto Pulse	1	Brass
H36LBHS227	VC33F	3/8" Cuno Gas Strainer	1	Brass
H36LBHS111	VC34F	3/16" O.D. Copper Tubing	20'	Copper
H36LBHS109	VC35F	3/16" Comp. Fitting & Nut	1	Brass
	VC36F	Ring Bracket (Cuno Strainer)	1	Brass
H36LBHS112	VC37F	5/16" O.D. Copper Tubing	5'	Copper
H36LBHS114	VC38F	5/16" Flared Tubing Nut	2	Brass
H36LBHS113	VC39F	5/16" x 1/4" Flared Ell	1	Brass
H36LBHS87	VC40F	1/4" Check Valve (Screwed)	2	Brass
H36LBHS116	VC41F	1/4" Overboard Fitting	1	Brass
H36LBHS237	VC42F	3" 12-V Exhaust Blower	2	Brass
H36LBHS210	VC43F	3" D x 30" 16 oz. Down-spout Tubing	2	Copper

PART #	FIGURE #	NAME	NO.REQD.	MATERIAL
H36LBHS211	VC44F	3" D 90° Downspout Ell (16 oz.)	2	Copper
H36LBHS62	VC45F	1-1/4" Bilge Strainer	1	Brass
H36LBHS50	VC46F	1-1/4" Bilge Strainer	1	Brass
H36LBHS351	VC47F	1-3/8" I.D.Radiator Hose	12"	Rubber
H36LBHS52	VC48F	1-3/4" Hose Clamps	8	Galv.
H36LBHS53	VC49F	1-1/4" Wrought 90° Ell (Sweat)	2	Copper
H36LBHS54	VC50F	1-1/4" I.D.Copper Tubing	6'9"	Copper
H36LBHS61	VC51F	1-1/4" Wrought 90° St. Ell	3	Copper
	VC52F	1-1/4" C x 1-1/4" S.P.S. Cast 90° Ell	1	Brass
H36LBHS146	VC53F	1-1/4" IN x 1-1/2" OUT Navy Type Hand Bilge Pump	1	Brass
H36LBHS29	VC54F	1-1/2" C x 1-1/2" S.P.S. Wrought Male Adapter	1	Brass
H36LBHS24	VC55F	1-1/2" I.D.Copper Tubing	39'9-1/2"	Copper
H36LBHS22	VC56F	1-5/8" I.D.Radiator Hose	49"	Rubber
H36LBHS23	VC57F	2" I.D.Hose Clamps	30	Galv.
H36LBHS115	VC58F	1-1/2" Overboard Fitting	3	Brass
H36LBHS55	VC59F	1-1/4" x 1-1/4" Wrought Male Adapter	1	Copper
H36LBHS63	VC60F	1-1/2" Bilge Strainer (End Connection)	1	Brass
	VC61F	1-1/2" Bilge Strainer (Top Connection)	1	Brass
H36LBHS64	VC62F	1-1/2" Check Valve (Sweat)	2	Brass
H36LBHS26	VC63F	1-1/2" Wrought 90° Ell (Sweat)	12	Copper
H36LBHS25	VC64F	1-1/2" Wrought 90° St. Ell (Sweat)	2	Copper
H36LBHS27	VC65F	1-1/2" Wrought 45° St. Ell (Sweat)		Copper
H36LBHS32	VC66F	1-1/2" 3-Way Cock (Screwed)	1	Brass
H36LBHS31	VC67F	1-1/2" x 1-1/2" Cast 90° Male Ell	3	Brass
H36LBHS28	VC68F	1-1/2" x 1-1/2" x 1/2" Cast Tee	1	Brass
H36LBHS221B	VC69F	Higgins Bilge Pump	1	Bronze
H36LBHS223	VC70F	1/2" x 3-1/2" Vee Groove Pulley	2	Steel
H36LBHS67	VC71F	1/2" I.D.Copper Tubing	7'2"	Copper
H36LBHS69	VC72F	5/8" I.D.Radiator Hose	16"	Copper
H36LBHS120	VC73F	1/2" Wrought Ell(Sweat)	4	Copper
	VC74F	48" Vulco Belt	1	
H36LBHS246	VC75F	1/8" x 1/8" x 2" Key Stock (PUMP PULLEY)	2	Brass

PART #	FIGURE #	NAME	NO.REQD.	MATERIAL
H36LBHS257	VC76F	13-1/2" of 3/16" x 6" Channel Iron	1	Galv.
	VC77F	1/2" Globe Valve (Sweat)	1	Brass
H36LBHS140	VC78F	2" D Cold Rolled Steel	2"	Steel
H36LBHS141	VC79F	1" D Cold Rolled Steel	7"	Steel
H36LBHS138	VC80F	1/2" x 1" Set Screw USS	1	Steel
H36LBHS139	VC81F	1/2" Lock Nut (USS)	1	Steel
	VC82F	Clutch Arm	1	Steel
H36LBHS150	VC83F	3/4" Female Clevis	2	Brass
H36LBHS151	VC84F	3/8" x 1-3/8" Clevis Pin	2	Cadm.Pl.
H36LBHS152	VC85F	3/32" x 1" Cotter Pins	2	Brass
H36LBHS99	VC86F	3/4" Cold Rolled Steel Rod (Thr.Both Ends SAE)	10"	Steel
H36LBHS153	VC87F	3/4" Male Rod End SAE	1	Brass
H36LBHS154	VC88F	3/4" Hex. Nuts S.A.E.	2	Steel
H36LBHS225	VC89F	Vacuum Power Cylinder	1	Steel
	VC90F	Vacuum Release Valve	1	Bronze
H36LBHS133	VC91F	1/8" Plugs (Screwed)	3	Galv.
H36LBHS224	VC92F	Vacuum Supply Tank	1	Galv.
H36LBHS72	VC93F	1/2" Close Nipple	3	Galv.
H36LBHS74	VC94F	1/2" Tee (Screwed)	1	Brass
H36LBHS121	VC95F	1/2" C x 1/2" P Wrought Male Adapter	3	Copper
H36LBHS122	VC96F	1/2" Check Valve (Sweat)	1	Brass
H36LBHS68	VC97F	1/2" Wrought 90° St. Ell	1	Copper
H36LBHS70	VC98F	7/8" I.D. Hose Clamps	4	Galv.
H36LBHS123	VC99F	3/4" C x 1/2" P Wrought Male Adapter	2	Copper
H36LBHS124	VC100F	3/4" I.D. Copper Tubing	52'	Copper
H36LBHS125	VC101F	7/8" I.D. Radiator Hose	24"	Rubber
H36LBHS126	VC102F	1-1/4" I.D.Hose Clamps	16	Galv.
H36LBHS127	VC103F	3/4" Wrought 90° St. Ell (Sweat)	2	Copper
H36LBHS129	VC104F	3/4" Wrought 45° Ell (Sweat)	3	Copper
H36LBHS128	VC105F	3/4" Wrought 90° Ell (Sweat)	23	Copper
H36LBHS135	VC106F	3/4" St. Ell (Screwed)	1	Galv.
	VC107F	3/4" Ell (Screwed)	1	Galv.
H36LBHS91	VC108F	1/2" Ell (Screwed)	1	Brass
H36LBHS78	VC109F	1/2" x 1/4" Bushing	1	Brass
	VC110F	1/2" C x 1/4" Cast 90° Male Ell	1	Brass
H36LBHS130	VC111F	3/4" Globe Valve Sweat	1	Brass
	VC112F	3/4" Close Nipple	1	Galv.
H36LBHS136	VC113F	3/4" x 3/4" Wrought Male Adapter	1	Copper
H36LBHS338	VC114F	Higgins Control Valve	1	Bronze
	VC115F	Clutch Lever Shaft Arm	1	Steel
H36LBHS186	VC116F	5/16" x 3/8" U.S.S. Bell Crank Complete	1	Brass
H36LBHS175	VC117F	5/16" U.S.S. Female Clevis, Pin & Key	2	Brass

PART #	FIGURE #	NAME	NO.REQD.	MATERIAL
H36LBHS188	VC118F	5/16" U.S.S.Ball Joint	1	Cad.Pl.
	VC119F	5/16" x 41-1/2" Brass Rod (Thr. Both Ends)	1	Brass
	VC120F	5/16" x 17" Brass Rod (Thr. Both Ends)	1	Brass
H36LBHS170	VC121F	2" #2 Arms	2	Brass
	VC122F	3/8" D x 3/4" Brass Pipe Spacer	2	Brass
H36LBHS174	VC123F	1/2" Pillow Blocks	2	Bronze
	VC124F	1/2" Brass Rod	36"	Brass
	VC125F	3/8" Brass Rod	42"	Brass
H36LBHS200	VC126F	3/8" Compensating Unit	1	Brass
H36LBHS188	VC127F	2" Scoop	1	Brass
H36LBHS1	VC128F	2" Thru Hull Fitting	1	Brass
H36LBHS5	VC129F	2" Gate Valve (Screwed)	1	Brass
H36LBHS4	VC130F	2" Close Nipple	1	Brass
H36LBHS2	VC131F	2" Plug (Screwed)	1	Brass
H36LBHS3	VC132F	2" Tee (Screwed)	1	Brass
H36LBHS7	VC133F	2" I.D.Copper Tubing	7'	Copper
H36LBHS9	VC134F	2-1/8" I.D.Radiator Hose	18"	Rubber
H36LBHS10	VC135F	2-1/2" I.D. Hose Clamps	12	Galv.
H36LBHS8	VC136F	2" Cast 90° Ell	4	Brass
H36LBHS6	VC137F	2" C x 2" S.P.S.Cast Male Adapter	3	Brass
H36LBHS15	VC138F	2" Wrought 90° Ell	3	Copper
	VC139F	1-1/4" x 1" x 2" Cast Tee	1	Brass
	VC140F	2" x 1-1/4" x 1" Wrought Tee		Brass
H36LBHS11	VC141F	2" C x 2" S.P.S. Cast Male Ell	2	Brass
H36LBHS43	VC142F	1" Wrought 90° St. Ell	6	Copper
H36LBHS45	VC143F	1-1/8" I.D.Radiator Hose	24"	Rubber
H36LBHS42	VC144F	1-1/2" I.D.Hose Clamps	16	Galv.
	VC145F	1" Wrought 90° Ell	12	Copper
H36LBHS44	VC146F	1" C x 1" S.P.S. Cast 90° Male Ell	5	Brass
H36LBHS14	VC147F	1/8" Petcock Drains	3	Brass
H36LBHS16	VC148F	2" x 3/4" x 2" Cast Tee	1	Brass
H36LBHS298	VC149F	3/4" Close Nipple	1	Brass
H36LBHS299	VC150F	3/4" Check Valve (Screwed)	1	Brass
H36LBHS18	VC151F	2" Sherwood Pump Flanges	2	Brass
	VC152F	54" Vulco Belts	2	Brass
H36LBHS219	VC153F	2" Sherwood Pump	1	Bronze
H36LBHS222	VC154F	7/8" x 7.2" Double Groove Pulley (Sherwood)	1	Steel
H36LBHS217	VC155F	2" Grass Trap (Gross Mech.Lab.)	1	Steel
	VC156F	1" Salt Water Inlet Flange	1	Bronze
	VC157F	1" x 2" x 1-1/2" Wrought Tee (Sweat)	1	Copper
	VC158F	Capital Vee Drive	1	Copper
	VC159F	Vee Drive Shaft	1	Steel

PART #	FIGURE #	NAME	NO.REQD.	MATERIAL
	VC160F	Oil Cooler & Strainer	1	Steel
	VC161F	Oil Sump Tanks	1	Steel
	VC162F	Oil Pump	1	Steel
	VC163F	4-1/2" x 40 Copper Exhaust	1	Copper
H36LBHS44	VC164F	1" C x 1" S.P.S. Cast Male Ell	1	Copper
H36LBHS233	VC165F	Brass Exh. Flange	1	Brass
H36LBHS34	VC166F	1-1/2" C x 1-1/4" P Cast Male Ell	1	Brass
H36LBHS80	VC167F	1-1/2" x 1-1/2" x 1/2" Dole "Plan" Thermostat	1	Brass
H36LBHS21	VC168F	1-1/2" C x 2" S.P.S. Cast Male Adapter	2	Brass
H36LBHS218	VC169F	2" Ross Heat Exchanger	1	
	VC170F	1-1/2" x 1-1/2" x 1/2" Wrought Tee	1	Copper
H36LBHS29	VC171F	1-1/2" C x 1-1/2" P Cast Male Adapter	1	Brass
H36LBHS221A	VC172F	Higgins Fresh Water Pump	1	Bronze
H36LBHS49	VC173F	47" Vulco Vee Belt	1	Bronze
H36LBHS47	VC174F	1-1/2" Raised Boss Flange	1	Brass
	VC175F	5/16" C x 1/8" P Flared Ell	3	Brass
	VC176F	5/16" C x 1/8" P Flared Half Union	1	Brass
H36LBHS114	VC177F	5/16" Flared Tubing Nuts	4	Brass
	VC178F	F. W. Exp. Tank	1	Galv.
H36LBHS161	VC180F	1/4" T x 1/8" P Flared Ell	2	Brass
H36LBHS162	VC181F	1/4" Flared Nuts	2	Brass
	VC182F	1/4" I.D. Radiator Hose	3"	Rubber
	VC183F	1/2" I.D. Hose Clamps	2	Galv.
H36LBHS92	VC184F	1/2" C x 3/8" P Cast Male Ell	1	Brass
	VC185F	Heat Indicator (Heat Indicator guage & line)	1	
	VC186F	2" D x 3-1/2" Wrought Iron Pipe (Crank Lever Sleeve)	1	
H36LBHS278	VC187F	Flywheel Pulley & Stub Shaft	1	
	VC188F	Tach. & Cable Complete With Housing	14'	
H36LBHS191	VC189F	1/2" Cleats	24	
H36LBHS235	VC190F	3/8" Cleats	24	
H36LBHS236	VC191F	1/4" Cleats	12	
H36LBHS212	VC192F	#5 Insulated Staples	1 Box.	
H36LBHS195	VC193F	#14 Galv.Uph.Tacks	6 Doz.	
H36LBHS300	VC194F	7/32" x 8" x 11" Sherwood Pump Plate	1	Galv.Iron
H36LBHS301	VC195F	3/16" x 3" x 11-1/4" S.W. Pump Adjusting Plate	1	Galv.Iron

PART #	FIGURE #	NAME	NO.REQD.	MATERIAL
H36LBHS273	VC196F	5/32" F. W. Pump Bracket	1	Galv.Iron
H36LBHS257	VC197F	Engine Bilge Pump Bracket (6" x 12-1/2" Channel)	1 pc.	Galv.Iron
H36LBHS249	VC198F	5/32" x 3-1/2" x 6" Gas Strainer Bracket	1	Galv.Iron
H36LBHS247	VC199F	5/32" x 2-1/2" x 6" Auto Pulse Bracket	1	Galv.Iron
H36LBHS254	VC200F	1/8" x 6-1/2" x 8" Ign. Coil Bracket	1	Galv.Iron
H36LBHS196	VC201F	1/4" x 1" U.S.S. Cap Screw	2	
H36LBHS275	VC202F	5/16" x 1" U.S.S. Cap Screw	8	
	VC203F	5/16" x 1-3/4" U.S.S.Cap Screw	4	
	VC204F	3/8" x 1-1/4" U.S.S. Cap Screw	4	
	VC205F	3/8" x 2-1/2" U.S.S. Cap Screw	2	
H36LBHS267	VC206F	1/2" x 1-1/2" Flat Head Cap Screws	4	
H36LBHS250	VC207F	10-24 x 3/4" F.H. Mach. Screw	6	Galv.
	VC208F	#8-32 x 3/4" R.H. Mach. Screw	1	Brass
H36LBHS194	VC209F	#10 x 1" R.H. Wood Screw	36	Brass
H36LBHS272	VC210F	#10 x 1" F.H. Wood Screw	72	Brass
H36LBHS248	VC211F	#14 x 1" F.H. Wood Screw	96	Brass
H36LBHS262	VC212F	#14 x 2" F.H. Wood Screw	48	Brass
H36LBHS251	VC213F	#10-24 Hex. Nuts	6	Galv.
H36LBHS179	VC214F	#12-24 Hex. Nuts	4	Brass
H36LBHS197	VC215F	1/4" St. Hex. Nut	2	Steel
H36LBHS276	VC216F	5/16" Std. Hex. Nut	13	Steel
H36LBHS268	VC217F	1/2" Std. Hex. Nut	4	Steel
	VC218F	3/8" Std. Hex. Nut	4	Steel
H36LBHS154	VC219F	3/4" S.A.E. Hex. Nut	2	Steel
	VC220F	#8-32" Hex. Nut	1	Brass
	VC221F	1/16" x 1/2" Cotter Key	12	Brass
H36LBHS155	VC222F	3/32" x 1/2" Cotter Key	2	Brass
H36LBHS152	VC223F	3/32" x 1" Cotter Key	3	Brass
	VC224F	3/32" x 1-1/4" Cotter Key	2	Brass
	VC225F	3/16" Lock Washers	6	Steel
H36LBHS253	VC226F	1/4" Lock Washers	3	Steel
H36LBHS189	VC227F	5/16" Lock Washers	16	
	VC228F	3/8" Lock Washers	6	
	VC229F	1/2" Lock Washers	5	
	VC230F	3/16" Flat Washers	6	
H36LBHS252	VC231F	1/4" Flat Washers	3	
	VC232F	5/16" Flat Washers	12	
H36LBHS180	VC233F	5/8" Flat Washers	3	
	VC234F	1" I.D. Copper Tubing	35'	
	VC235F	1/2" Wrought Tee	1	Copper
	VC236F	1-1/4" 3-Way Cock (Screwed)	1	Brass
	VC237F	2" Check Valve (Sweat)	1	Brass
	VC238F	Instrument Panel	1	
	VC240F	1" Globe Valve (Sweat)	1	Brass

APPENDIX B

36ft Ramp Type Eureka Landing Boat. Hall-Scott Engine Installation. Fresh Water or Salt Water Cooled with V-Drive. (Ref 1)

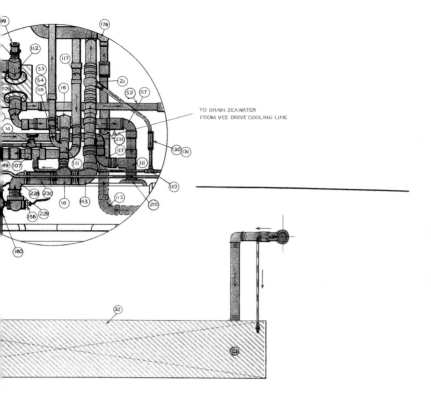

TO DRAIN SEAWATER
FROM VEE DRIVE COOLING LINE

NOTE

FOR PARTS AND PRICE LIST REFER
TO SECTION VII OF SUPPLEMENT
TO PARTS CATALOG No. 106,
TITLED HIGGINS INSTALLATION
HALL SCOTT MOTOR 36' VEHICLE
CARRIER FRESH AND SALT WATER
COOLED.

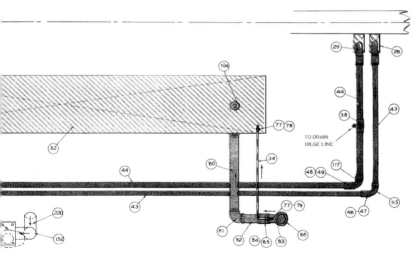

TO DRAIN
BILGE LINE

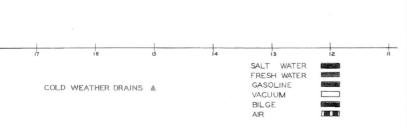

COLD WEATHER DRAINS

SALT   WATER
FRESH WATER
GASOLINE
VACUUM
BILGE
AIR

HIGGINS INDUSTRIES, INC.
521 CITY PARK AVENUE
NEW ORLEANS, LA., U.S.A.

36 FT. RAMP TYPE
EUREKA LANDING BOAT
HALL   SCOTT   INSTALLATION
FRESH OR SALT WATER COOLED

DRAWN BY: A.B. TATE	DATE: 9-17-41
TRACED BY: J.V. MONTZ & HYMEL	SCALE: 1½"-1'-0"
CHECKED BY:	JOB NO:
APPROVED BY:	CONTRACT NO:
FILE NO. W-277	DWG. NO. 2585-7D

Parts List

Figure number VC-1 refers to item 1 in the diagram on the previous page.

PART #	FIGURE #	NAME	REQUIRED	MATERIAL
H36LBHS218	VC-1	Ross Heat Exchange	1	Brass
H36LBHS217	VC-2	Grass Trap Gross 2"	1	Bronze
H36LBHS228	VC-3	Higgins Remote Control Actuator Valve	1	Bronze
H36LBHS219	VC-4	Sherwood Pump 2" Openings	1	Bronze
H36LBHS221A	VC-5	Higgins Bronze Pump Bilge, Type "B"	1	Bronze
H36LBHS221B	VC-6	Higgins Bronze Pump Fresh Water, Type "B"	1	Bronze
H36LBHS237	VC-7	Blower 12-V	2	Alum.
H36LBHS224	VC-8	Vacuum Surge Tank	1	Galv.Iron
H36LBHS225	VC-9	Vacuum Power Cylinder	1	
H36LBHS238	VC-10	Auto Pulse	1	
H36LBHS227	VC-11	Cuno Gas Strainer 3/8" Openings	1	
H36LBHS141	VC-12	Clutch Shaft Extension 1" Dia. x 7" L.	1	Steel
H36LBHS146	VC-13	Navy Type Hand Bilge Pump	1	Brass
H36LBHS71	VC-14	1/2" Gate Valve Sweat	1	Brass
H36LBHS122	VC-15	1/2" Check Valve	1	Brass
	VC-16	1-1/2" 3-Way Valve	3	Brass
H36LBHS32	VC-17	Fresh Water Expansion Tank	1	Copper
	VC-18	Fresh Water Fill Cap on Engine		
H36LBHS130	VC-19	Vacuum Shut Off Valve	1	Brass
	VC-20	Throttle Offset Connecting Rod 5/16" x 41-1/2"	1	Brass
H36LBHS80	VC-21	Dole Plan Thermostat	1	Alum.
H36LBHS5	VC-22	2" Gate Valve Sea Water Intake	1	Brass
	VC-23	4-1/8" Dia. Exhaust Pipe	1	Copper
H36LBHS13	VC-24	2" Check Valve Sweat Type	1	Brass
H36LBHS62	VC-25	Bilge Strainer Top Connection	1	Brass
H36LBHS113	VC-26	Bilge Overboard Discharge 1-1/2"	1	Brass
H36LBHS116	VC-27	Carburetor Overboard Discharge 1/4"	1	Brass
H36LBHS50	VC-28	Bilge Strainer End Connection 1-1/4"	1	Brass
H36LBHS63	VC-29	Bilge Strainer End Connection 1-1/2"	1	Brass
H36LBHS	VC-30	1/2" Flared Tubing Nuts	6	Brass
	VC-31	Vee Drive	1	
	VC-32	Gasoline Tanks	2	St. Steel
	VC-33			
	VC-34	3/8" O.D. Copper Tubing	20'	Copper
H36LBHS115	VC-35	Salt Water Overboard Discharge 1-1/2"	1	Brass
H36LBHS87	VC-36	1/4" Swing Check Valve	3	Brass
H36LBHS107	VC-37	1/4" Ball Check Valve	1	Brass
H36LBHS64	VC-38	1-1/2" Swing Check Valve Sweat	2	Brass

PART #	FIGURE #	NAME	REQUIRED	MATERIAL
H36LBHS299	VC-39	3/4" Swing Check Valve	1	Brass
H36LBHS226A	VC-40	Vacuum Release Valve	1	Bronze
H36LBHS56	VC-41	1-1/4" 3-Way Cock Screwed		Brass
H36LBHS124	VC-42	3/4" Tubing	52'	Copper
H36LBHS54	VC-43	1-1/4" Tubing	44'	Copper
H36LBHS24	VC-44	1-1/2" Tubing	42"	Copper
H36LBHS7	VC-45	2" Tubing	9"	Copper
H36LBHS51	VC-46	1-3/8" I.D. Radiator Hose	2'	Rubber
H36LBHS52	VC-47	1-3/4" Hose Clamps	16	Galv.Iron
H36LBHS22	VC-48	1-5/8" I.D. Radiator Hose	4'8"	Rubber
H36LBHS23	VC-49	2" Hose Clamps	23	Galv.Iron
H36LBHS9	VC-50	2-1/8" I.D. Radiator Hose	1'4"	Rubber
H36LBHS10	VC-51	2-1/2" Hose Clamps	7	Galv.Iron
H36LBHS41	VC-52	1" Tubing	6'	Copper
H36LBHS45	VC-53	1-1/8" I.D. Radiator Hose	6"	Rubber
H36LBHS42	VC-54	1-1/2" Hose Clamps	4	Galv.Iron
H36LBHS125	VC-55	7/8" I.D. Radiator Hose	2'	Rubber
H36LBHS126	VC-56	1-1/4" Hose Clamps	16	Galv.Iron
	VC-57	Connecting Rod 5/16" x 17-1/2"	1	Brass
H36LBHS48	VC-58	Vulco Belt 54"	2	Rubber
	VC-59	Vulco Belt 48"	1	Rubber
H36LBHS49	VC-60	Vulco Belt 47"	1	Rubber
H36LBHS175	VC-61	5/16" Clevis	3	Brass
H36LBHS174	VC-62	1/2" Pillow Blocks	2	Bronze
H36LBHS186	VC-63	5/16" x 2" x 2" x 3/8" Bell Crank	1	Brass
H36LBHS190	VC-64	Arm 2"	2	Brass
	VC-65	Connecting Rod 36" x 1/2"	1	Brass
H36LBHS142	VC-66	1" Pillow Block	1	Bronze
	VC-67	3/4" x 1/2" Spacer	2	Brass
H36LBHS194	VC-68	#10 x 1" Rd. Head Brass Wood Screws	36	Brass
H36LBHS158	VC-69	Brass Discs 3/16" x 1-1/2" Dia.	2	Brass
H36LBHS188	VC-70	5/16" Ball Joint	1	Brass
H36LBHS150	VC-71	3/4" Clevis	2	Brass
H36LBHS99	VC-72	Connecting Rod 3/4" x 10"	1	Steel
H36LBHS153	VC-73	Male Rod End 3/4"	1	Brass
H36LBHS278	VC-74	Fly Wheel Shaft Extension	1	Steel
	VC-75	Vee Drive Higgins Joint	1	
	VC-76	Handles for Gasoline Shut Off Valve 5/16" x 19"	2	Brass
H36LBHS82	VC-77	3/8" Flared Tubing Nuts	14	Brass
H36LBHS81	VC-78	3/8" T x 1/4" SPS Flared Elbows	8	Brass
H36LBHS88	VC-79	3/8" T x 1/4" SPS Half Union	4	Brass
	VC-80	19" x 2" Nipple	2	Galv.Iron
	VC-81	2" 90° Elbow	2	Galv.Iron
	VC-82	30" x 2" Pipe Thread One End	2	Galv.Iron
H36LBHS214	VC-83	8" x 2" Pipe Thread One End	2	Brass

PART #	FIGURE #	NAME	REQUIRED	MATERIAL
H36LBHS215	VC-84	6" x 2-3/8" I.D. Radiator Hose	2	Rubber
H36LBHS258	VC-85	Hose Clamps 2-3/4"	4	Galv. Iron
H36LBHS216	VC-86	2" Protecto Seal	2	Brass
H36LBHS68	VC-87	1/2" Street Elbows	2	Brass
H36LBHS94	VC-88	1/2" x 3/8" Bushings	2	Brass
H36LBHS95	VC-89	3/8" x 2" Close Nipple	2	Brass
H36LBHS96	VC-90	3/8" Gas Valves	2	Brass
H36LBHS97	VC-91	1/2" T x 3/8" P Flared Elbow	3	Brass
H36LBHS100	VC-92 VC-93	1/2" Flared Tee	1	Brass
H36LBHS84	VC-94	3/8" x 1/4" Brass Bushings	1	Brass
	VC-95	1/4" Close Nipple	1	Brass
H36LBHS85	VC-96 VC-97 VC-98	1/4" Tee Screwed	1	Brass
H36LBHS109	VC-99	3/16" T x 1/8" P Comp. Half Union & Nut	1	Brass
	VC-100	3/16" O.D. Tubing	19'	Brass
H36LBHS113	VC-101	5/16" T x 1/4" P Flared Elbow	1	Brass
H36LBHS114	VC-102	5/16" Flared Tubing Nut	2	Brass
H36LBHS112	VC-103	5/16" O.D. Copper Tubing	5'	Copper
H36LBHS83	VC-104	1-1/2" Pipe Plugs	2	Brass
	VC-105	1-1/2" Bilge Strainer Top Connection	1	Brass
H36LBHS159	VC-106	#12-24 Hex. Nuts	4	Brass
H36LBHS28	VC-107	1-1/2" C x 1-1/2" C x 1/2" C Tee	2	Brass
H36LBHS74	VC-108	1/2" Tee Screwed Brass	3	Brass
H36LBHS3	VC-109	2" Tee Screwed	1	Brass
H36LBHS89	VC-110	1/2" Tee Sweat	2	Copper
H36LBHS36	VC-111	1-1/2" Tee Wrought	2	Copper
H36LBHS16	VC-112	2" x 3/4" x 2" Cast Tee	1	Copper
H36LBHS37	VC-113	2" x 1-1/2" x 1" Cast Tee	1	Copper
	VC-114	1-1/4" x 1-1/4" x 2" Wrought Tee	2	Copper
H36LBHS53	VC-115	1-1/4" 90° Wrought Elbow		Copper
H36LBHS57	VC-116	1-1/4" 90° Street Elbow		Copper
H36LBHS26	VC-117	1-1/2" 90° Elbow Wrought		Copper
H36LBHS25	VC-118	1-1/2" 90° Street Elbow	3	Copper
H36LBHS27	VC-119	1-1/2" 45° Street Elbow	3	Copper
H36LBHS43	VC-120	1" 90° Wrought Elbow	3	Copper
H36LBHS118	VC-121	1" 45° Wrought Elbow	1	Copper
	VC-122	1/2" x 3-1/2" Single Groove Pulley	2	Steel
H36LBHS222	VC-123	7/8" x 7.2" Double Groove Pulley	1	Steel
H36LBHS128	VC-124	3/4" 90° Wrought Elbow	18	Brass
H36LBHS127	VC-125	3/4" 90° Street Elbow	2	Brass
H36LBHS129	VC-126	3/4" 45° Wrought Elbow	3	Brass
H36LBHS1	VC-127	1/2" Wrought Street Elbow 90°	2	Brass

PART #	FIGURE #	NAME	REQUIRED	MATERIAL
	VC-128	1/2" Wrought Elbow 90°	3	Brass
H36LBHS67	VC-129	1/2" I.D. Copper Tubing	12'2"	Copper
H36LBHS69	VC-130	5/8" I.D. Radiator Hose	22"	Rubber
H36LBHS70	VC-131	1" Hose Clamps	16	Galv.Iron
H36LBHS133	VC-132	1/8" Pipe Plug	3	Galv.Iron
H36LBHS135	VC-133	3/4" Street Elbows Screwed	2	Galv.Iron
H36LBHS136	VC-134	3/4" C x 3/4" SPS Wrought Male Adapter	2	Brass
H36LBHS135	VC-135	1/2" Elbow	1	Brass
H36LBHS72	VC-136	1/2" Close Nipple	1	Brass
H36LBHS108	VC-137	1/4" x 1/8" Bushing	1	Brass
	VC-138	2" x 2" Cold Rolled Steel	1	Steel
H36LBHS67	VC-139	5/8" O.D. Tubing	12'	Copper
	VC-140	1-1/4" C x 1-1/4" SPS Cast Male Elbow	1	Copper
	VC-141	1-1/2" C x 1-1/2" SPS Wrought Male Adapter	1	Copper
H36LBHS55	VC-142	1-1/4" C x 1-1/4" SPS Wrought Male Adapter	1	Copper
H36LBHS31	VC-143	1-1/2" C x 1-1/2" SPS Cast Male Elbow	4	Copper
H36LBHS29	VC-144	1-1/2" C x 1-1/2" SPS Wrought Male Adapter	1	Copper
H36LBHS21	VC-145	1-1/2" C x 2" SPS Cast Male Adapter	2	Copper
H36LBHS6	VC-146	2" C x 2" SPS Cast Male Adapter	3	Copper
H36LBHS1	VC-147	2" Overboard Fitting	1	Brass
H36LBHS8	VC-148	2" Cast 90° Elbow	8	Copper
H36LBHS29	VC-149	1-1/2" C x 1-1/2" SPS Cast Male Adapter	1	Copper
	VC-150	3/4" C x 1/2" SPS Cast Male Adapter	1	Copper
H36LBHS55	VC-151	1-1/4" C x 1-1/4" SPS Cast Male Adapter	2	Copper
H36LBHS211	VC-152	3" Down Spout Elbow	2	Copper
H36LBHS153	VC-153	3/4" Male Rod End SAE	1	Bronze
H36LBHS154	VC-154	3/4" Hex. Nuts SAE	2	Steel
H36LBHS200	VC-155	Compensating Unit	1	Brass
	VC-156	Connecting Rod Compensating Unit 3/8" x 37-1/4"	1	Brass
H36LBHS11	VC-157	2" C x 2" SPS Cast Male Elbows	2	Brass
	VC-158	Heat Indicator Element	1	
H36LBHS72	VC-159	1/2" Close Nipple	1	Galv.Iron
H36LBHS121	VC-160	1/2" C x 1/2" SPS Adapter	3	Copper
H36LBHS123	VC-161	3/4" C x 1/2" SPS Adapter	1	Copper
H36LBHS161	VC-162	1/4" x 1/8" Flared Elbow	2	Brass
H36LBHS162	VC-163	1/4" Flared Nut	2	Brass
	VC-164	1/2" x 1/8" Pipe Bushing	1	Brass
H36LBHS191	VC-165	1/2" Brass Cleats	24	Brass
H36LBHS235	VC-166	3/8" Brass Cleats	24	Brass
H36LBHS236	VC-167	1/4" Brass Cleats	12	Brass
H36LBHS212	VC-168	#5 Insulative Staples	1 Bx.	
	VC-169	Brass Ring Bracket for Cuno Gas Strainer	1	Brass

PART #	FIGURE #	NAME	REQUIRED	MATERIAL
H36LBHS196	VC-170	1/4" x 1" Cap Screw	2	Steel
H36LBHS275	VC-171	5/16" x 1" Cap Screw	8	Steel
	VC-172	5/16" x 1-3/4" Cap Screw	4	Steel
	VC-173	3/8" x 1-1/4" Cap Screw	4	Steel
	VC-174	3/8" x 2-1/2" Cap Screw	2	Steel
H36LBHS267	VC-175	1/2" x 1-1/2" Flat Head Cap Screw	4	Steel
H36LBHS250	VC-176	#10-24 x 3/4" F.H. Galv. Machine Screws	6	Galv.Iron
	VC-177	#8-32 x 3/4" Rd. Head Brass Machine Screws	1	Brass
	VC-178	2" x 1-1/4" x 1-1/4" Tee Wrought	1	Copper
H36LBHS272	VC-179	#10 x 1" Flat Head Wood Screws	6	Bronze
H36LBHS248	VC-180	#14 x 1" Flat Head Wood Screws	8	Bronze
H36LBHS262	VC-181	#14 x 2" Flat Head Wood Screws	4	Bronze
H36LBHS251	VC-182	#10-24 Galv. Hex. Nuts	6	Galv.Iron
H36LBHS179	VC-183	#12-24 Brass Hex. Nuts	4	Brass
H36LBHS197	VC-184	1/4" Standard Hex. Nuts	2	Brass
H36LBHS276	VC-185	5/16" Standard Hex. Nuts	13	Brass
H36LBHS268	VC-186	1/2" Standard Hex. Nuts	4	Steel
	VC-187	3/8" Standard Hex. Nuts	4	Steel
	VC-188	#8-32" Brass Hex. Nuts	1	Brass
	VC-189	3/16" Lock Washers	6	Steel
H36LBHS253	VC-190	1/4" Lock Washers	3	Steel
H36LBHS189	VC-191	5/16" Lock Washers	16	Steel
	VC-192	3/8" Lock Washers	6	Steel
	VC-193	1/2" Lock Washers	5	Steel
	VC-194	3/16" Flat Washers	6	Galv.Iron
H36LBHS252	VC-195	1/4" Flat Washers Galv.	3	Galv.Iron
	VC-196	5/16" Flat Washers Galv.	12	Galv.Iron
H36LBHS180	VC-197	5/8" Galv. Flat Washers	3	Galv.Iron
	VC-198	1/16" x 1/2" Brass Cotter Key	12	Brass
H36LBHS155	VC-199	3/32" x 1/2" Brass Cotter	3	Brass
H36LBHS152	VC-200	3/32" x 1" Brass Cotter Key	3	Brass
H36LBHS	VC-201	3/32" x 1-1/4" Steel Cotter Key	2	Steel
H36LBHS300	VC-202	Sherwood pump plate 7/32" x 8" x 11" Galv.	1	Galv.Iron
H36LBHS301	VC-203	Salt Water Pump Adjustment Plate 3/16" x 3" x 11-1/4" Galv.	1	Galv.Iron
H36LBHS273	VC-204	Fresh Water Pump Bracket	1	Galv.Iron
H36LBHS300	VC-205	Engine Bilge Pump Bracket 6" x 12-1/2" Galv.	1	Galv.Iron
H36LBHS249	VC-206	Gasoline Strainer Bracket 6/32" x 3-1/2" x 6" Galv.	1	Galv.Iron

PART #	FIGURE #	NAME	REQUIRED	MATERIAL
H36LBHS247	VC-207	Auto Pulse Bracket 5/32" x 2-1/2" x 6" Galv.	1	Galv.Iron
H36LBHS254	VC-208	Ignition Coil Bracket 1/8" x 6-1/2" x 8" Galv.	1	Galv.Iron
H36LBHS18	VC-209	2" Sherwood Pump Flanges	2	Galv.Iron
H36LBHS47	VC-210	Water Inlet Flange Bossed 1-5/8"	1	Galv.Iron
H36LBHS233	VC-211	Brass Exhaust Pipe Flange 4-1/8" Dia.	1	Brass
H36LBHS147	VC-212	Tachometer Complete with Cables	1	Brass
H36LBHS165	VC-213	Instrument Panel	1	
H36LBHS238	VC-214	3-1/2" of 2" Steel Pipe for Hand Crank	1	Steel
H36LBHS246	VC-215	Key for Double Groove Pulley	2	Steel
H36LBHS246	VC-216	Key for Single Groove Pulley	1	Steel
H36LBHS149	VC-217	Hall Scott Tachometer Adapter 2-1	1	
	VC-218	Gasoline Fill Cap 2"	2	Bronze
H36LBHS151	VC-219	3/8" x 1-3/8" Cadium Clevis Pin	2	Steel
H36LBHS210	VC-220	3" Down Spout Tubing 30"	2	Copper
H36LBHS138	VC-221	1/2" x 1" Set Screw	1	Steel
H36LBHS139	VC-222	1/2" Lock Nut	1	Steel
H36LBHS137	VC-223	1/4" x 1" Woodruff Key	1	Steel
H36LBHS4	VC-224	2" Close Nipple	1	Brass
H36LBHS2	VC-225	2" Pipe Plug	1	Brass
H36LBHS298	VC-226	3/4" Close Nipple	1	Brass
H36LBHS44	VC-227	1" C x 1" SPS Cast Male Elbow	1	Brass
H36LBHS34	**VC-228**	1-1/2" x 1-1/4" Reducing Elbow Screwed	1	Brass
H36LBHS35	VC-229	1-1/4" Close Nipple	1	Brass
H36LBHS33	VC-230	1-1/2" x 6" Nipple	1	Brass
H36LBHS27	VC-231	1-1/2" Wrought 45° Elbow	3	Brass
	VC-232	1" Globe Valve (Sweat)	1	Brass
H36LBHS284	VC-236	4 Groove Pulley 1-5/8" Shaft 7.2" O.D. Fly Wheel	1	Steel

APPENDIX C   **Superior Diesel Engine 36ft Eureka Landing Boat with Direct Drive. (Ref 1)**

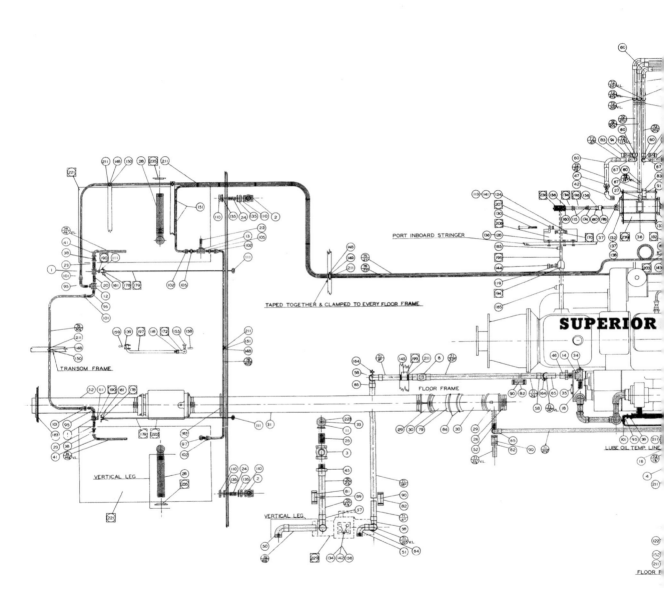

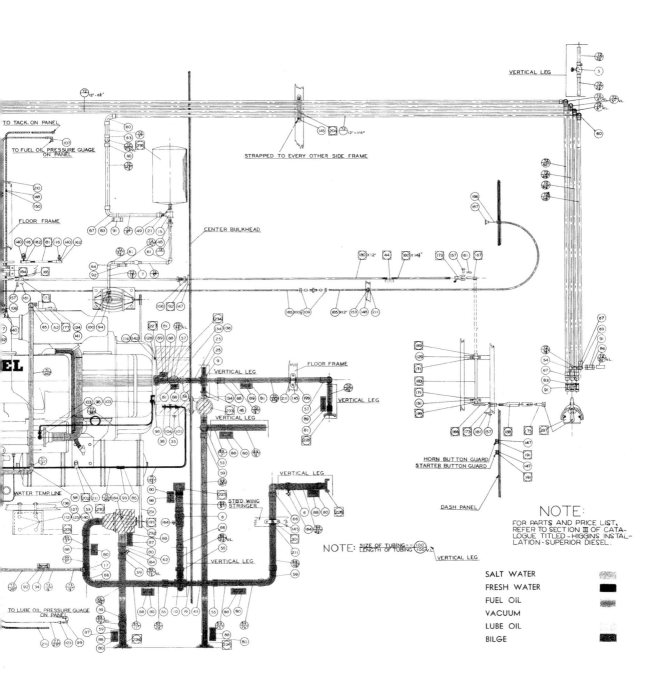

NOTE:
FOR PARTS AND PRICE LIST,
REFER TO SECTION III OF CATA-
LOGUE TITLED –HIGGINS INSTAL-
LATION–SUPERIOR DIESEL.

NOTE: SIZE OF TUBING-- (100)
LENGTH OF TUBING (100) V.L.

SALT WATER
FRESH WATER
FUEL OIL
VACUUM
LUBE OIL
BILGE

PART #		NAME	NUMBER REQ.	MATERIAL
H36LBS	1	3/8" Gas Valve(Screwed)	2	Brass
H36LBS	2	3/4" Gate Valve (Screwed)	2	Brass
H36LBS	3	1-1/4" Gate Valve (Screwed)	1	Brass
H36LBS	4	1/2" Gate Valve(Sweat)	1	Brass
H36LBS	5	3/4" Globe Valve(Sweat)(With Drain)	1	Brass
H36LBS	6	1-1/2" Swing Check(Sweat) (Horizontal)	1	Brass
H36LBS	7	1/2" Swing Check (Sweat)	1	Brass
H36LBS	8	1" Swing Check (Sweat) (Horizontal)	1	Brass
H36LBS	9	1-1/4" Three Way Cock(Screwed)	1	Brass
H36LBS	10	1-1/2" Three Way Cock(Screwed)	1	Brass
H36LBS	11	1-1/4" Tee (Screwed)	1	Brass
H36LBS	12	3/8" Tee (Screwed)	1	Brass
H36LBS	13	1/4" Tee (Screwed)	1	Brass
H36LBS	14	1" Tee (Screwed)	1	Brass
H36LBS	15	1/2" Tee (Screwed)	1	Brass
H36LBS	16	1" x 1"x 1/2" Wraught Tee (Sweat)	1	Brass
H36LBS	17	1-1/2"x 1-1/2"x 1/2" Cast Tee (Sweat)	1	Brass
H36LBS	18	1" Close Nipple (Screwed)	1	Brass
H36LBS	19	1/2" Close Nipple (Screwed)	1	Brass
H36LBS	20	3/8" Close Nipple (Screwed)	1	Brass
H36LBS	21	1/2" Close Nipple (Screwed)	1	Galv.Iron
H36LBS	22	1/4" Close Nipple (Screwed)	1	Brass
H36LBS	23	3/8" x 2" Nipple (Screwed)	2	Brass
H36LBS	24	3/4" x 3" Nipple (Screwed)	2	Brass
H36LBS	25	1-1/4" x 2-1/2" Nipple(Screwed)	3	Brass
H36LBS	26	3" I.P.S. x 4" Nipple(Screwed)	1	Black Iron
H36LBS	27	1/2" x 4" Nipple (Screwed)	1/2 to a boat	Galv.Iron
H36LBS	28	2" x 26" Nipple(Thread both ends)(Screwed)	2	
H36LBS	29	3"I.D. 45° Elbow (Screwed)	2	Black Iron
H36LBS	30	3"I.D.x9" Nipple (Screwed)	2	Black Iron
H36LBS	31	3" I.D. x 81" Exhaust Pipe	1	Black Iron
H36LBS	32	3" I.D. x 36" Exhaust Pipe	1	Black Iron
H36LBS	33	1-1/4" Sq.Hd. Pipe Plug (Screwed)	1	Brass
H36LBS	34	1" Sq. Head Pipe Plug (Screwed)	1	Brass
H36LBS	35	1/2" Sq. Head Pipe Plug (Screwed)	3	Brass
H36LBS	36	1/2" Sq. Head Pipe Plug (Screwed)	1	Galv.Iron
H36LBS	37	1/8" Sq. Head Pipe Plug (Screwed)	2	Galv.Iron
H36LBS	38	1/2" x 3/8" Bushing(Screwed)	3	Brass
H36LBS	39	1/2" x 1/4" Bushing(Screwed)	1	Brass
H36LBS	40	1/8" x 1/4" Bushing(Screwed)	1	Brass
H36LBS	41	1/4" Strut Ells (Screwed)	2	Brass
H36LBS	42	3/4" Strut Ells (Screwed)	2	Galv.Iron
H36LBS	43	1-1/2" Pipe Coupling(Screwed)	1	Brass

PART #		NAME	NUMBER REQ.	MATERIAL
H36LBS	44	3/8" Rod Coupling (Screwed)	1	Brass
H36LBS	45	1-1/4"C x 1-1/2" S.P.S. Wrought Male Adapter	2	Copper
H36LBS	46	1"C x 1" S.P.S. Wrought Male Adapter	1	Copper
H36LBS	47	3/4"C x 3/4" S.P.S. Wrought Male Adapter	2	Copper
H36LBS	48	1/2"C x 1/2" S.P.S. Wrought Male Adapter	1	Copper
H36LBS	49	3/4"C x 1/2" S.P.S. Wrought Male Adapter	1	Copper
H36LBS	50	1-1/4" C x 1-1/4" S.P.S. Cast Male 90° ell	1	Brass
H36LBS	51	1"C x 1-1/4" S.P.S. Cast Male 90° ell	1	Brass
H36LBS	52	1"C x 1" S.P.S. Cast Male 90° ell	2	Brass
H36LBS	53	1-1/2" C x 1-1/2"S.P.S. Cast Male 90° ell	2	Brass
H36LBS	54	3/4"C x 1/2" S.P.S. Cast Male 90° ell	1	Brass
H36LBS	55	1-1/2"C x 1-1/2" S.P.S. Cast Male 90° ell	3	Brass
H36LBS	56	1-1/4" C x 1-1/4" S.P.S. Cast Female Adapter	1	Brass
H36LBS	57	1-1/4" Wrought 90° ell (Sweat)	3	Copper
H36LBS	58	1" Wrought 90° ell (Sweat)	4	Copper
H36LBS	59	1-1/2" Wrought 90° ell (Sweat)	5	Copper
H36LBS	60	3/4" Wrought 90° ell (Sweat)	21	Copper
H36LBS	61	1/2" Wrought 90° ell (Sweat)	2	Copper
H36LBS	62	1-1/2" Wrought 45° ell (Sweat)	1	Copper
H36LBS	63	3/4" Wrought 45° ell (Sweat)	5	Copper
H36LBS	64	1" Wrought 45° St. ell (Sweat)	1	Copper
H36LBS	65	1" Wrought 45° St. ell (Sweat)	4	Copper
H36LBS	66	1-1/2" Wrought 90° St.ell (Sweat)	3	Copper
H36LBS	67	3/4" Wrought 90° St. ell (Sweat)	8	Copper
H36LBS	68	1-1/4" Wrought 90° St.ell (Sweat)	2	Copper
H36LBS	69	1-1/2" I.D. Copper Tubing	10'8-1/4"	
H36LBS	70	1-1/4" I.D. Copper Tubing	77-1/4"	Copper
H36LBS	71	1" I.D. Copper Tubing	139-1/2"	Copper
H36LBS	72	3/4" I.D. Copper Tubing	95'	Copper
H36LBS	73	1/2" I. D. Copper Tubing	75-3/8"	Copper
H36LBS	74	3/8" I. D. Copper Tubing	29"	Copper
H36LBS	75	3/8" O. D. Copper Tubing	28-1/4"	Copper
H36LBS	76	5/16"O. D. Copper Tubing	20'6-1/2"	Copper
H36LBS	77	1/4" O. D. Copper Tubing	28'	Copper
H36LBS	78	1/8" O. D. Copper Tubing	25'	Copper
H36LBS	79	3-1/2" I. D. 4 Ply Condor Hose	6"	
H36LBS	80	1-5/8" I. D. Radiator Hose	29"	
H36LBS	81	1-3/8" I. D. Radiator Hose	29"	
H36LBS	82	1-1/8" I. D. Radiator Hose	15"	

PART #	NAME	NUMBER REQ.	MATERIAL
H36LBS 83	7/8" I.D. Radiator Hose	8"	
H36LBS 84	5/8" I.D. Radiator Hose	22"	
H36LBS 85	3/8" I.D. Radiator Hose	8"	
H36LBS 86	#25-3M4" Galv. Hose Clamps	2	Galv. Iron
H36LBS 87	2-1/2" I.D. Galv. Hose Clamps	2	Galv. Iron
H36LBS 88	2" I.D. Galv. Hose Clamps	18	Galv. Iron
H36LBS 89	1-3/4" I.D. Galv. Hose Clamps	8	Galv. Iron
H36LBS 90	1-1/2" I.D. Galv. Hose Clamps	6	Galv. Iron
H36LBS 91	1-1/4" I.D. Galv. Hose Clamps	16	Galv. Iron
H36LBS 92	7/8" I.D. Galv. Hose Clamps	6	Galv. Iron
H36LBS 93	5/8" I.D. Galv. Hose Clamps	2	Galv. Iron
H36LBS 94	5/8" T x 1/2" P Flared Elbow	1	Brass
H36LBS 95	3/8" T x 3/8" P Flared Type Elbow	4	Brass
H36LBS 96	3/8" T x 1/4" P Flared Type Elbow	1	Brass
H36LBS 97	5/16" T x 1/4" P Flared Type Elbow	2	Brass
H36LBS 98	1/4" T x 1/8" P. Flared Type Elbow	2	Brass
H36LBS 99	1/4" T x 1/8" P Flared Type Elbow	1	Brass
H36LBS 100	5/8" Flared Type Nuts	1	Brass
H36LBS 101	3/8" Flared Type Tubing Nuts	6	Brass
H36LBS 102	5/16" Flared Type Tubing Nuts	4	Brass
H36LBS 103	1/4" Flared Type Tubing Nuts	3	Brass
H36LBS 104	3/8" T x 1/4" P Flared Type Half Union	1	Brass
H36LBS 105	5/16" T x 1/4" P Flared Type Half Union	2	Brass
H36LBS 106	1/8" T x 1/8" P Ferrule Type Ell and Nut	1	Brass
H36LBS 107	1/8" T x 1/8" P Ferrule Type Female Ell and Nut #70F	1	Brass
H36LBS 108	7/16" T x 1/4" P Ferrule Type Half Union	1	Brass
H36LBS 109	3/16" Comp. Type Full Union	1	Brass
H36LBS 110	3/4" Pipe Lock Nuts	4	Brass
H36LBS 111	#12-24 Hex Nuts	4	Brass
H36LBS 112	5/16" U.S.S. Hex Nuts	4	Steel
H36LBS 113	3/8" U.S.S. Hex Nuts	2	Steel
H36LBS 114	1/4" S.A.E. Hex Nuts	6	Steel
H36LBS 115	3/4" S.A.E. Hex Nuts	2	Steel
H36LBS 116	5/16" S.A.E. Hex Nuts	2	Steel
H36LBS 117	3/8" U.S.S. Hex Lock Nuts	3	Steel
H36LBS 118	5/8" S.A.E. Hex Nuts	1	Steel
H36LBS 119	1/2" U.S.S. Hex Lock Nut	1	Steel
H36LBS 120	3/16" U.S.S. Galv. Sq. Nut	1	Steel
H36LBS 121	3/16" x 7/8" U.S.S. Flathead Galv. Mach. Screw	1	Steel
H36LBS 122	3/16" x 1/2" U.S.S. Round Head Mach. Screw	1	Steel
H36LBS 123	8/32" x 1/4" U.S.S. Round Head Mach. Screw	1	Steel

PART #	NAME	NUMBER REQ.	MATERIAL
H36LBS 124	3/8" x 1-1/4" U.S.S. Hex Hd. Cap Screws	4	Steel
H36LBS 125	5/16" x 1" U.S.S. Hex Hd. Cap Screws	4	Steel
H36LBS 126	1/4" x 1" S.A.E. Hex Head Cap Screws	6	Steel
H36LBS 127	1/4" x 3-1/2" Galv. Carriage Bolts and Nuts	4	Galv.Iron
H36LBS 128	1/4" x 2-1/2" Galv. Carriage Bolts and Nuts	3	Galv.Iron
H36LBS 129	1/4" x 2-1/4" Galv. Carriage Bolts and Nuts	2	Galv.Iron
H36LBS 130	3/8" x 5" Galv. Carriage Bolts and Nuts	1	Galv.Iron
H36LBS 131	1/4" x 4" Galv. Carriage Bolts and Nuts	2	Galv.Iron
H36LBS 132	3/8" x 4" Galv. Carriage Bolts and Nuts	2	Galv.Iron
H36LBS 133	3/8" x 2-1/2" Galv. Carriage Bolts and Nuts	2	Galv.Iron
H36LBS 134	1/4" x 1-1/2" Galv. Carriage Bolts and Nuts	12	Galv.Iron
H36LBS 135	1" Flat Washer	4	Brass
H36LBS 136	1/4" Flat Washer Galv.	21	Galv.Iron
H36LBS 137	3/8" Flat Washer Galv.	4	Galv. Iron
H36LBS 138	1/2" Flat Washer Galv.	4	Galv.Iron
H36LBS 139	5/8" Flat Washer Galv.	2	Steel
H36LBS 140	5/16" Lock Washers	6	Steel
H36LBS 141	3/8" Lock Washers	4	Steel
H36LBS 142	1/4" Lock Washers	6	Steel
H36LBS 143	3/8" x 2" U.S.S. Set Screws	1	Steel
H36LBS 144	1/2" x 1-1/4" U.S.S. Set Screws	1	Steel
H36LBS 145	#10 x 3/4" Round Head Wood Screws	16	Brass
H36LBS 146	#14 x 2-1/2" Flat Head Wood Screws	4	Brass
H36LBS 147	#6 x 5/8" Flat Head Wood Screws	10	Brass
H36LBS 148	5/8-10 Oz.Tacks for Piping Cleats	124	Steel
H36LBS 149	1/2" Pipe Cleats	8	Brass
H36LBS 150	3/8" Pipe Cleats	30	Brass
H36LBS 151	5/16" Pipe Cleats	3	Brass
H36LBS 152	1/4" Pipe Cleats	12	Brass
H36LBS 153	3/16" Pipe Cleats	38	Brass
H36LBS 154	# 5 Insulated Staples	16	Copper
H36LBS 155	5/8" x 1-3/4" Steel Construction Rivet	1	Steel
H36LBS 156	3/8" x 1-3/8" Clevis Pin (Cad. Plated)	2	Steel
H36LBS 157	5/16" x 1" Clevis Pin (Cad.Plated)	3	Steel
H36LBS 158	3/16" x 1-1/2" Cotter Pin	1	Brass
H36LBS 159	1/8" x 1-1/2" Cotter Pin	1	Brass
H36LBS 160	3/32" x 1" Cotter Pins	2	Brass

PART #	NAME	NUMBER REQ.	MATERIAL
H36LBS 161	3/32" x 1/2" Cotter Pins	7	Brass
H36LBS 162	5/16" S.A.E. Ball Joint (Cad.Plated)	2	Steel
H36LBS 163	3-1/2" Galv. Flange (Exhaust)	2	Iron
H36LBS 164	1/8" Pet Cock Drain (Screwed)	6	Brass
H36LBS 165	1/4" x 1-1/4" Woodruff Keys	2	Steel
H36LBS 166	#25 Arm (Trottle)	1	Brass
H36LBS 167	#14 Arm (Trottle)	2	Brass
H36LBS 168	#13 Arm (Trottle)	1	Brass
H36LBS 169	1/4" x 3/8" Rivet (Engine Stop)	1	Steel
H36LBS 170	1" Pillow Block	1	Bronze
H36LBS 171	1/2" Pillow Block	4	Bronze
H36LBS 172	5/8" Female Clevis	1	Brass
H36LBS 173	3/8" Female Clevis	3	Brass
H36LBS 174	3/4" Female Clevis	2	Brass
H36LBS 175	Compensating Unit	1	Brass
H36LBS 176	3/4" Male Rod End (SAE)	1	Brass
H36LBS 177	Cast Brass Flange	1	Brass
H36LBS 178	1/4" D x 3-1/2" Connecting Rod	2	Brass
H36LBS 179	5/16" D x 56" Connecting Rod	2	Brass
H36LBS 180	3/8" D x 13" 2-1/2" Connecting Rod	1	Brass
H36LBS 181	5/16" D x 8-1/2" Connecting Rod (Thread both ends SAE)	1	Brass
H36LBS 182	3/8" D x 1" Rod	1	Brass
H36LBS 183	1/2" D x 22-3/4" Connecting Rod	1	Brass
H36LBS 184	1/2" D x 4-1/2" Connecting Rod	1	Brass
H36LBS 185	3/16" D Tubing	22-1/2'	Brass
H36LBS 186	Choke Wire # 16 Ga. B & S	23'	Brass
H36LBS 187	Engine Stop Handle (Choke Handle)	1	
H36LBS 188	3/8" D x 43" Pipe	1	Brass
H36LBS 189	3/8" x 3/4" Pipe Spacer	2	Brass
H36LBS 190	3/16" x 1-1/2" D Disc	2	Brass
H36LBS 191	1/8" x 1" x 3" Brass Plates	2	Brass
H36LBS 192	1/8" x 2" x 2" Brass Plates	1	Brass
H36LBS 193	1/8" x 1/8" x 2" Key Stock	1	Brass
H36LBS 194	2" of 2" D. Cold Rolled Steel	1	Steel
H36LBS 195	13" of 1" D. Cold Rolled Steel	1	Steel
H36LBS 196	11" of 3/4" D Cold Rolled Steel	1	Steel
H36LBS 197	5/8" D x 35-1/2" D Cold Rolled Steel	1	Steel
H36LBS 198	3/8" D x 2-1/2" Galv. Rod	1	Iron
H36LBS 199	3/4" x 5-18 Ga. Galv. Strap Iron	2	Galv. Iron
H36LBS 200	3/4" x 8" 18 Ga. Galv. Strap Iron	1	Galv. Iron
H36LBS 201	3/4" x 5-3/4" 18 Ga. Galv. Strap Iron	1	Galv. Iron
H36LBS 202	3/4" x 3" 18 Ga. Galv. Strap Iron	1	Galv. Iron
H36LBS 203	3/16" x 3/4" x 9-1/2" Galv. Iron (Engine Stop)	1	Iron
H36LBS 204	1" x 7-24 Ga. Galv. Strap Iron	5	Iron
H36LBS 205	10" of 1/8" x 3/4" Galv. Iron	1	Galv.Iron
H36LBS 206	11" of 1/4" x 3" x 3-1/2" Galv. Angle Iron	1	Galv.Iron
H36LBS 207	4" of 1/4" x 2" x 2" Galv. Angle Iron	1	Galv.Iron

PART #	NAME	NUMBER REQ.	MATERIAL
H36LBS 208	1/4" x 3" x 10" Flat Iron	1	Galv.Iron
H36LBS 209	9" of 3" x 6" Channel Iron	1	Galv.Iron
H36LBS 210	Tack (Complete):2" 1-28'	1	
H36LBS 211	#1/2 Roll 3/4" Black Friction Tape	1	
H36LBS 212	1/32" Gasket Material	9 sq.in.	
H36LBS 213	# 25 Brazing Rod	1	
H36LBS 214	Acid Core Solder	1/4 LB	
H36LBS 215	Hard Solder 95-5	2 LBS.	
H36LBS 216	Perfecto Seal (Pipe Dope)	2 ozs. 1 Tube	
H36LBS 217	Scotch Masking Tape 60 yd. Roll	1/8	
H36LBS 218	Nokorode 2 Ounce Can	1-1/2	
H36LBS 219	White Lead (For Exhaust)		
H36LBS 220	Gray Engine Enamel (Half Pt.Can)	1/8	
H36LBS 221	Monel Fuel Tanks	2	Monel
H36LBS 222	Maxim Exhaust Silencer	1	
H36LBS 223	1-1/4" Overboard Fitting	1	Brass
H36LBS 224	1-1/2" Overboard Fitting	2	Brass
H36LBS 225	1-1/2" Bilge Strainer(End Hose Connection)	1	Brass
H36LBS 226	1-1/4" Bilge Strainer (Top Hose Connection)	1	Brass
H36LBS 227	1-1/4" Bilge Strainer (End Hose Connection)	1	Brass
H36LBS 228	1-1/2" Bilge Strainer (Top Hose Connection)	1	Brass
H36LBS 229	1-1/4" Duplex Grass Trap	1	
H36LBS 230	Higgins Bronze Water Pump (1-1/2" Intake-1-1/4" Outlet)	1	Bronze
H36LBS 231	#3520 Vulco Belt	1	
H36LBS 232	1/2" x 3-1/2" Single Grove Vee Pulley	1	
H36LBS 233	Navy Type Hand Bilge Pump (1-1/4" Intake-1-1/2"Outlet)	1	
H36LBS 234	Copper E x P Tank (Comes with Engine)	1	
H36LBS 235	2" Deck Plates (Mark "Fuel")	2	Brass
H36LBS 236	Clutch Trigger Ensembly (Made Up)	1	
H36LBS 237	Clutch and Trottle Control Valve	1	
H36LBS 238	Vacuum Tank (Single Connection)	1	
H36LBS 239	Clutch Power Cylinder	1	
H36LBS 240	Fwd. Throttle Offset		
H36LBS 241	Aft. Throttle Offset		

APPENDIX D   **Gray Marine Diesel Engine Installation with Direct Drive.
(Ref 1)**

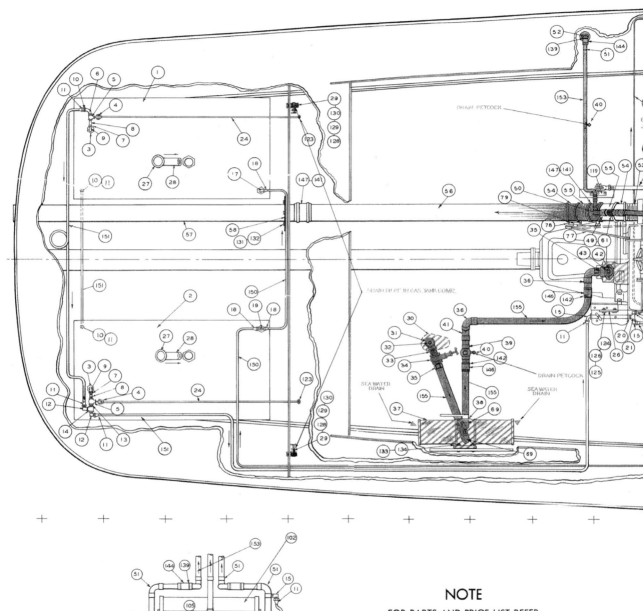

NOTE

FOR PARTS AND PRICE LIST REFER
TO SECTION X OF SUPPLEMENT
TO PARTS CATALOG No. 106,
TITLED HIGGINS INSTALLATION
GRAY MARINE DIESEL ENGINE.

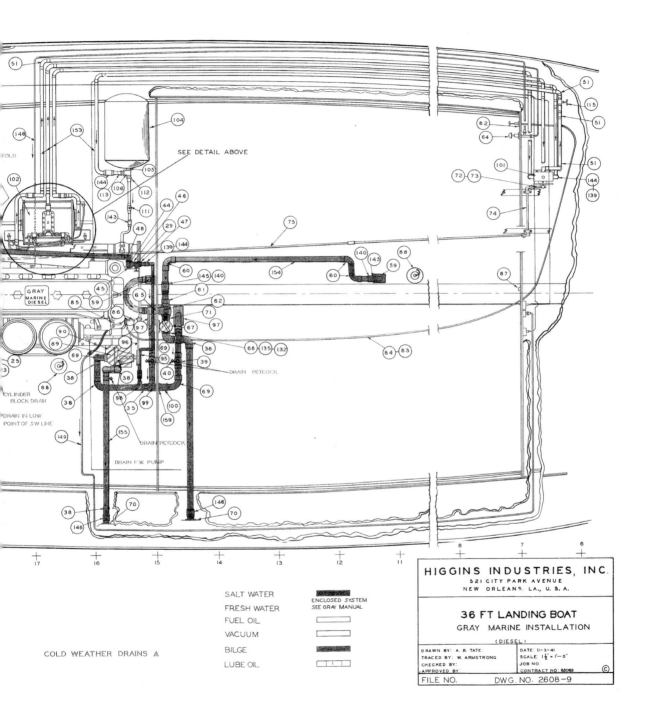

SALT WATER

FRESH WATER

FUEL OIL

VACUUM

BILGE

LUBE OIL

COLD WEATHER DRAINS ⚠

HIGGINS INDUSTRIES, INC.
521 CITY PARK AVENUE
NEW ORLEANS, LA., U. S. A.

36 FT LANDING BOAT

GRAY MARINE INSTALLATION

(DIESEL)

DRAWN BY: A. B. TATE	DATE: 11-3-41
TRACED BY: W. ARMSTRONG	SCALE: 1½" = 1'-0"
CHECKED BY:	JOB NO:
APPROVED BY:	CONTRACT NO: 85066
FILE NO.	DWG. NO. 2608-9

PART #	NAME	NO.REQD.	MATERIAL
H36LBGMD-1	Fuel Tank (Port)	1	Monel
H36LBGMD-2	Fuel Tank (Strbd.)	1	Monel
H36LBGMD-3	Fuel Tank Syphon Line	2	Copper
H36LBHMD-4	3/16" x 1-1/2" Brass Disc	2	Brass
H36LBGMD-5	3/8" Globe Valve (Screwed)	2	Brass
H36LBGMD-6	3/8" St. Ell(Screwed)	1	Brass
H36LBGMD-7	1/2" x 3/8" Bushing (Screwed)	2	Brass
H36LBGMD-8	3/8" x 2" Pipe Nipple	2	Brass
H36LBGMD-9	1/2" St. Ell (Screwed)	2	Brass
H36LBGMD-10	3/8" x 3/8" Flared Half Union	3	Brass
H36LBGMD-11	3/8" Flared Tubing Nut	14	Brass
H36LBGMD-12	3/8" x 3/8" Flared Ell	2	Brass
H36LBGMD-13	3/8" Close Nipple	1	Brass
H36LBGMD-14	3/8" Pipe Tee (Screwed)	1	Brass
H36LBGMD-15	3/8" T x 1/4" P Flared Ell	10	Brass
H36LBGMD-16	3/8" x 3/8" Full Union (Flared)	1	Brass
H36LBGMD-17	5/16" T x 1/4" P Flared Ell	1	Brass
H36LBGMD-18	5/16" Flared Tubing Nut	4	Brass
H36LBGMD-19	5/16" T x 5/16" T x 1/4" P Flared Tubing Tee	1	Brass
H36LBGMD-20	1/4" Close Nipple	7	Brass
H36LBGMD-21	1/4" Tee (Screwed)	3	Brass
H36LBGMD-22	1/4" T x 1/4" P Flared Ell	1	Brass
H36LBGMD-23	1/4" Flared Tubing Nuts	1	Brass
H36LBGMD-24	Fuel Valve Ext. Handle	2	Brass
H36LBGMD-25	5/16" x 5/16" Full Union	1	Brass
H36LBGMD-26	Purolator Bracket	1	Galv.Iron
H36LBGMD-27	2" Deck Plate (Mark "Fuel")	2	Brass
H36LBGMD-28	2" I.D. x 24" Galv.Iron Nipple	2	Galv.Iron
H36LBGMD-29	3/4" Gate Valve (Screwed)	3	Brass
H36LBGMD-30	1-1/2" Salt Water Scoop Strainer	1	Brass
H36LBGMD-31	1-1/2" Tee (Screwed)	1	Brass
H36LBGMD-32	1-1/2" Plug (Sq.Hd.)	1	Brass
H36LBGMD-33	1-1/2" Close Nipple	3	Brass
H36LBGMD-34	1-1/2" Gate Valve (Screwed)	1	Brass
H36LBGMD-35	1-1/2" C x 1-1/2" SPS Cast Male Adapter	5	Brass
H36LBGMD-36	1-1/2" 90° Wrought St. Ell	4	Copper
H36LBGMD-37	1-1/2" Duplex Grass Trap	1	
H36LBGMD-38	1-1/2" 90° Wrought Ell	4	Copper
H36LBGMD-39	1-1/2" Swing Check	3	Brass
H36LBGMD-40	1/8" Petcock Drain (Screwed)	5	Brass
H36LBGMD-41	1-1/2" 45° Wrought Ell (Sweat)	1	Copper
H36LBGMD-42	3/4" Coupling (Screwed)	1	Brass
H36LBGMD-43	3/4" Sq. Hd. Pipe Plug	1	Brass
H36LBGMD-44	1-1/4" x 1-1/4" x 3/4" Tee (Screwed)	1	Brass
H36LBGMD-45	1-1/4" Close Nipple	1	Brass
H36LBGMD-46	3/4" Close Nipple	2	Brass
H36LBGMD-47	3/4" C x 3/4" P Cast Male Adapter	1	Brass
H36LBGMD-48	1-1/4" C x 1-1/4" P Cast Male Ell	1	Brass

PART #	NAME	NO.REQD.	MATERIAL
H36LBGMD-49	1-1/4" x 3/4" x 3/4" Tee (Screwed)	1	Brass
H36LBGMD-50	3/4" C x 3/4" P Cast Male Ell	1	Brass
H36LBGMD-51	3/4" Wrought 90° Ell	21	Copper
H36LBGMD-52	3/4" Overboard Fitting	1	Brass
H36LBGMD-53	4" I.D. x 4" Pipe Nipple	1	Black Iron
H36LBGMD-54	4" I.D. 45° Ell	2	Black Iron
H36LBGMD-55	4" I.D. x 7" Pipe (Thr. one End)	2	Black Iron
H36LBGMD-56	4" I.D. x 63" Pipe (Thr. one End)	1	Black Iron
H36LBGMD-57	4" I.D. x 63" Pipe	1	Black Iron
H36LBGMD-58	4-1/2" I.D. Thr. Bulkhd. Exh. Flange	1	Galv.Iron
H36LBGMD-59	1-1/4" Bilge Strainers (End Connection)	2	Brass
H36LBGMD-60	1-1/4" Wrought 90° Ell	3	Copper
H36LBGMD-61	1-1/4" C x 1-1/4" P Cast Male Adapter	1	Brass
H36LBGMD-62	1-1/4" 3-Way Cock (Screwed)	1	Brass
H36LBGMD-63	1-1/4" Close Nipple	1	Brass
H36LBGMD-64	Primer Unit (With Engine)	1	Brass
H36LBGMD-65	1-1/4" C x 1-1/4" P Wrought Female Adapter	1	Copper
H36LBGMD-66	1-1/4" x 2-1/2" Nipple	2	Brass
H36LBGMD-67	1-1/4" in x 1-1/2" Out Navy Type Hand Bilge Pump	1	Brass
H36LBGMD-68	Hand Bilge Pump Bracket	2	Brass
H36LBGMD-69	1-1/2" C x 1-1/2" P Cast Male Ell	4	Brass
H36LBGMD-70	1-1/2" Overboard Fitting	2	Brass
H36LBGMD-71	1-1/4" St. Ell (Screwed)	1	Brass
H36LBGMD-72	Compensating Unit	1	Brass
H36LBGMD-73	Remote Control Spring Tension Rod, Comp. Unit Conn. Rod.	1	Brass
H36LBGMD-74	Throttle Offset Unit	1	Brass
H36LBGMD-75	3/8" Throttle Linkage	1	Brass
H36LBGMD-76	3/8" U.S.S. Male Clevis Pin & Key	2	Brass
H36LBGMD-77	5/16" Throttle Linkage Connecting	1	Brass
H36LBGMD-78	Throttle Bell Crank Unit	1	Brass
H36LBGMD-79	Throttle Bell Crank Bracket	1	Galv.Iron
H36LBGMD-80	1/4" x 1" Cap Screws	2	Steel
H36LBGMD-81	#14 x 1" F.H. Wood Screws	4	Brass
H36LBGMD-82	Engine Stop Handle (With Engine)	1	Brass
H36LBGMD-83	16 ga. x 25' Brass Spring Wire	1	Brass
H36LBGMD-84	3/16" x 24' Brass Housing	1	Brass
H36LBGMD-85	Engine Stop Unit	1	Brass
H36LBGMD-86	Housing Clamp Unit	1	Brass
H36LBGMD-87	Starter Button Guard	1	Brass
H36LBGMD-88	1-1/4" Garboard Drain Plug	2	Brass
H36LBGMD-89	Higgins Bilge Pump	1	Bronze
H36LBGMD-90	Higgins Bilge Pump Bracket	1	Galv.Iron
H36LBGMD-91	5/16" Lock Washers	4	Steel
H36LBGMD-92	5/16" Flat Washers	4	Steel

PIECE #	NAME OF PIECE	NO. REQD.	MATERIAL
H36LBGMD-93	5/16" x 1" Cap Screws	4	Steel
H36LBGMD-94	#14 x 2" F. H. Wood Screws	4	Brass
H36LBGMD-95	1/2" x 3-1/2" Vee Pulley	1	Steel
H36LBGMD-96	Vulco 3510 Vee Belt (Gates)	1	
H36LBGMD-97	1-1/2" Bilge Strainers (End Connection)	2	Brass
H36LBGMD-98	1-1/2" x 1-1/2" x 3/4" Cast Tee	1	Brass
H36LBGMD-99	1-1/2" 3-Way Cock (Screwed)	1	Brass
H36LBGMD-100	1-1/2" Coupling (Screwed)	1	Brass
H36LBGMD-101	Higgins Clutch & Throttle Control Valve	1	Bronze
H36LBGMD-102	Higgins Power Cylinder	1	Bronze
H36LBGMD-103	Higgins Power Cylinder Release Valves	2	Brass
H36LBGMD-104	Vacuum Surge Tank	1	Galv. Iron
H36LBGMD-105	1/2" Close Nipple	4	Brass
H36LBGMD-106	1/2" Tee (Screwed)	2	Brass
H36LBGMD-107	1/2" x 1/4" Bushing	2	Brass
H36LBGMD-108	1/4" Check Valve	4	Brass
H36LBGMD-109	1/2" x 1/2" Flared Tubing Ell	1	Brass
H36LBGMD-110	1/2" Tubing Nut (Flared)	1	Brass
H36LBGMD-111	1/2" Swing Check (Sweat)	1	Brass
H36LBGMD-112	1/2" C x 1/2" SPS Wrought Male Adapter	1	Copper
H36LBGMD-113	3/4" C x 1/2" SPS Wrought Male Adapter	1	Copper
H36LBGMD-114	3/4" Wrought 90° Ell	19	Copper
H36LBGMD-115	3/4" Globe Valve (Sweat)	1	Brass
H36LBGMD-116	3/4" S.A.E. Male Rod End	1	Brass
H36LBGMD-117	3/4" S.A.E. Clevis Pin & Key	2	Brass
H36LBGMD-118	3/4" Cyl. to Clutch Rod 10" SAE	1	Cold Rolled Steel
H36LBGMD-119	1" Pillow Block	1	Bronze
H36LBGMD-120	5/16" x 4-1/2" Carriage Bolts	2	Galv. Iron
H36LBGMD-121	5/16" x 5-1/2" Carriage Bolts	2	Galv. Iron
H36LBGMD-122	5/16" Flat Washers	4	Galv. Iron
H36LBGMD-123	12-24 Hex. Nuts	2	Brass
H36LBGMD-124	1/2" x 1-1/2" Cap Screws (Std.)	4	Steel
H36LBGMD-125	1/2" Hex. Nuts (Std.)	4	Steel
H36LBGMD-126	1/2" Lock Washers	4	Steel
H36LBGMD-127	#14 x 1" F. H. Wood Screws	2	Brass
H36LBGMD-128	3/4" 3" Pipe Nipple	2	Brass
H36LBGMD-129	1" Flat Washer	4	Brass
H36LBGMD-130	3/4" Pipe Lock Nuts	4	Brass
H36LBGMD-131	1/4" x 1-1/2" Carriage Bolts	4	Galv. Iron
H36LBGMD-132	1/4" Flat Washers	10	Galv. Iron
H36LBGMD-133	1/2" Flat Washers	3	Galv. Iron
H36LBGMD-134	1/2" x 2-1/2" Carriage Bolts	3	Galv. Iron
H36LBGMD-135	1/4" x 2" Carriage Bolts	6	Galv. Iron
H36LBGMD-136	1/2" Pipe Cleats	20	Brass
H36LBGMD-137	1/4" Pipe Cleats	20	Brass
H36LBGMD-138	7/8" Hose Clamps	2	Galv. Iron
H36LBGMD-139	1" Hose Clamps	24	Galv. Iron

PIECE #	NAME OF PIECE	NO.REQD.	MATERIAL
H36LBGMD-140	1-3/4" Hose Clamps	10	Galv.Iron
H36LBGMD-141	#28 Hose Clamps	4	Galv.Iron
H36LBGMD-142	2" Hose Clamps	18	Galv.Iron
H36LBGMD-143	5/8" Radiator Hose	3"	Rubber
H36LBGMD-144	7/8" Radiator Hose	36"	Rubber
H36LBGMD-145	1-3/8" Radiator Hose	16"	Rubber
H36LBGMD-146	1-5/8" Radiator Hose	29"	Rubber
H36LBGMD-147	4-1/2" I.D. Radiator Hose (4 Ply)	10"	Rubber
H36LBGMD-148	3/16" O.D. Tubing	24'	Copper
H36LBGMD-149	1/4" O.D. Tubing	50'	Copper
H36LBGMD-150	5/16" O.D. Tubing	18'	Copper
H36LBGMD-151	3/8" O.D. Tubing	28'	Copper
H36LBGMD-152	1/2" I.D. Tubing	6'	Copper
H36LBGMD-153	3/4" I.D. Tubing	100'	Copper
H36LBGMD-154	1-1/4" I.D. Tubing	11'	Copper
H36LBGMD-155	1-1/2" I.D. Tubing	17'	Copper
H36LBGMD-156	1-1/4" St. Ell (Screwed)	1	Brass
H36LBGMD-157	1/2" Ell (Screwed)	1	Brass
H36LBGMD-158	3/4" C x 1/2" SPS Cast Male Ell	1	Brass
H36LBGMD-159	1-1/2" Close Nipple	1	Brass

References

1. *Operator's Manual: Eureka Landing Motor Boats*, Higgins Industries, December 1941
2. F W Beasecker Papers (RHC-29), Special Collections, Grand Valley State University Libraries, Allendale, Michigan
3. *Instruction Manual: Gray Marine Diesels*, Detroit Diesel Engine Corporation, 1943
4. *Engineer Amphibian Troops*, Engineer Amphibian Command, US Army, 1943
5. *Skill in the Surf: A Landing Boat Manual*, Bureau of Naval Personnel, 1945
6. *Marine Engineman's Handbook*, TC 55-209, Department of the Army, 2009
7. Jerry E Strahan, *Andrew Jackson Higgins and the Boats That Won World War II*, Louisiana State University Press, Baton Rouge, 1994
8. Douglas Philips-Birt, *Sailing Yacht Design*, Adlard Coles Ltd, London, 1966
9. Courtesy of the National WWII Museum, New Orleans
10. Roberts Collection
11. *Characteristics of Japanese Naval Vessels: Article 10 Landing Craft*, US Naval Technical Mission to Japan, February 1946
12. US Utility Patent 2341866
13. Courtesy of John Posusta
14. *Motor Boating*, August 1937
15. George W Rappleyea, *Navigation Wrinkles for Combat Motor Boats*, Higgins Industries, 1943
16. US Marine Corps Archives, Quantico, Virginia
17. Norman Friedman, *US Amphibious Ships and Craft*, Naval Institute Press, Annapolis, Maryland, 2002
18. Al Adcock, *WWII US Landing Craft in Action*, Squadron/Signal Publications, Carrollton, Texas, 2003
19. Francis H Bradford, and Ric A Dias, *Hall-Scott: The Untold Story of a Great American Engine Maker*, SAE International, Warrendale, Pennsylvania, 2007
20. Robert Coram, 'The Bridge to the Beach', *World War II* magazine, Leedsburg, Pennsylvania, November/December 2010
21. US Marine Corps Archives, Quantico, Virginia via *World War II* magazine
22. Laughlin Collection
23. US Navy, *Instruction Manual: Superior SMRA-4, Superior Engine*, Holmesburg, Philadelphia, Pennsylvania, no date (circa 1942-1943)
24. *Motor Boating*, April 1934
25. David D Jackson, 'The US/American Automobile Industry in World War Two', http://usautoindustryworldwartwo.com
26. National Archives and Records Administration, Washington, DC
27. Edwin J Zufelt, *The Odyssey of the 411 Engineer Base Shop Battalion, 1943–1944: A Pictorial Narrative of the 411th Engineer Base Shop Battalion in Australia and New Guinea* (1945), World War Regimental Histories, Book 117; download from http://digicom.bpl.lib.me.us/ww_reg_his/117
28. *Motor Boating* magazine, July 1937
29. *The Rudder* magazine, January 1942
30. *The Rudder* magazine, October 1942
31. *Motorboat* magazine, November 1943
32. *Motor Boating* magazine, December 1943
33. Antony S Mollica, *Building Chris-Craft*, Voyageur Press, Minneapolis, Minnesota, 2010
34. Dave Gerr, *The Propeller Handbook*, McGraw-Hill Education, Blacklick, Ohio, 2001
35. *Professional Boat Builder* Magazine, August/September 1998, Issue #54
36. Norman Nudelman (Editor), *The Masthead*, Westlawn Institute of Marine Technology, June 2008
37. Detroit Diesel, Engine Specification 35A48, 1969
38. Linda Alvers, Executive Producer, *The Return of LST 325*
39. K C Barnaby, *Basic Naval Architecture*, Hutchinson, London, 1949
40. *Instruction Manual: Series 60 Marine Transmissions*, Bureau of Ships, US Navy
41. Courtesy of William Dvorak family
42. Department of Defense Navy Photo 58920
43. Charles C Roberts, Jr, *Armored Strike Force: The Photo History of the American 70th Tank Battalion in World War II*, Stackpole Books, Mechanicsburg, Pennsylvania, 2016
44. Wyatt Blassingame, *The US Frogmen of World War II*, Random House, New York, 1964
45. *Weapon Mounts for Secondary Armament*, Ordnance Corps, Detroit Arsenal Report, Contract No. DA-20-089-ORD-36713
46. US Army TM 9-230
47. Rendering courtesy of Alejandro Raigorodsky. Renderings © 2015 Alejandro Raigorodsky (used with permission)
48. *Motor Boating* magazine, January 1941